KEEPING COOL

WHEN THE HEAT IS ON

Bob Heil

Keeping Cool When the Heat is On

Bob Heil

Formerly: *Lessons from the Furnace*

Copyright © 1989 by Bob Heil
Printed in the United States of America
ISBN: 0-88368-205-2

Editorial assistance for Whitaker House by Debra Petrosky

Unless otherwise noted, Bible quotations are taken from the *King James Version*. Quotations identified NKJV are taken from the *New King James Version,* copyright © 1979, 1980, 1982, Thomas Nelson Inc., Publishers.

Acknowledgments

This book is the handiwork of God weaving the skills of many people together. *He* should get the acknowledgment and thanks. But God labors through human hands, and He desires thanks to be given wherever due. I consider it a joyous privilege to publicly thank those who labored with me.

Much thanks to my mother Anne for all the hours she spent typing and retyping the manuscript in each of its stages.

I give very special thanks to my wife Letitia who is a helpmeet indeed. The Lord has enabled her to write in a concise and interesting way. She faithfully labored with this talent during the years it took the book to come into being.

Finally, along the way the Lord sent many who were just the help needed at the moment. Much thanks for their faithfulness.

Table of Contents

INTRODUCTION

Are You an Overcomer?

I know many people who loathe their sins and themselves. Given the chance they would literally walk through a burning fiery furnace if it would cleanse them of their gripping sins. Because of tenacious guilt, these believers are weak and defeated in their Christian walk.

They fall into a sin, get up again, and run back to the cross. With tears and agony these tormented believers call out to God to forgive them: "I am ashamed; I am sorry. I never want to do that again. I will be faithful. Please wash this sin away in the blood of Jesus."

After rising from their knees, these Christians grit their teeth and set themselves once again not to fail. Their promises, good intentions, and will power may last three whole days before they fall into the same old sin. Once again they come weeping back to the cross. And once again Jesus forgives. Then they go on their way only to repeat the same pitiful process.

That is a sickeningly frustrating way to live. I know. I have been there. Surely there is a better way.

Ruling Your Own Spirit

Some wonder, why bother? Why is it so important to overcome sin; to overcome the frustrations and pressures of life; to overcome our own fleshly nature? I'm on my way to heaven. Why should I try to rise above my sins?

A very wise man once said,

> He that ruleth his spirit is better than he
> that taketh a city—Proverbs 16:32.

In the New Testament, the believer who rules his own spirit is known as an *overcomer,* and the heavenly blessings apply only to those who meet certain standards.

The blessings of the overcomer are spelled out in Revelation, chapters two and three. Jesus says, "To him that overcometh will I give to eat of the tree of life, which is in the midst of the paradise of God" (Revelation 2:7). This tree is given to all who are saved—to all born-again Christians who hold fast their confession to the end. All are to eat of this tree. But it goes further.

Jesus goes on to say that "he that overcometh shall not be hurt of the second death" (Revelation

2:11). Here we begin to see a distinction between Christians.

Some believers have not ruled their spirits. They have not overcome the sin in their lives. Their works have been wood and hay and stubble—not gold and silver. (See 1 Corinthians 3:11-15.) Although they are saved, they are hurt by the second death. Their works are burned up and not counted in the sight of God for eternal blessings.

A New Name

The greatest rewards are promised to those who overcome. Jesus says, "To him that overcometh will I give to eat of the hidden manna, and will give him a white stone, and in the stone a new name written, which no man knoweth saving he that receiveth it" (Revelation 2:17).

In Bible times people were given names that meant something. These were not just descriptive nicknames like "Red" or "Slim" but names that often contained deep spiritual significance. Many times special names were given because of special events, times, or places.

When Abram was seventy-five, God called him to leave his country and his father's house. He promised to bless Abram's descendants. Yet, at the age of ninety-nine, Abram was still childless. God reaffirmed His covenant with Abram and promised to greatly multiply him.

> As for me, behold, my covenant is
> with thee, and thou shalt be a father of
> many nations.
> Neither shall thy name any more be
> called Abram [Exalted Father], but thy
> name shall be Abraham [Father of a Mul-
> titude]; for a father of many nations have
> I made thee—Genesis 17:4,5.

God gave Abram a new name to symbolize the covenant He had made with him.

Jacob, one of the patriarchs of Israel, stole his brother Esau's blessing. Years later Esau and a band of four hundred men traveled to meet the conniving brother. Fearing revenge from his brother, Jacob divided his companies, spent the night in prayer, and even wrestled with an angel.

> And he [the angel] said unto him, What
> is thy name? And he said, Jacob. And he
> said, Thy name shall be called no more
> Jacob [Deceitful], but Israel [Prince with
> God]: for as a prince hast thou power
> with God and with men, and hast pre-
> vailed—Genesis 32:27,28.

Jacob's name was changed to represent the new character God was building in him.

In Revelation chapter two, God says He is going to give you a new name. Not just any old name. But a name that will symbolize a certain concept or truth. When God thinks of that truth or that strength, He will think of you. He will write it in a stone. And this will be your precious name, between Him and you alone. Oh, I want to be an overcomer.

The promises continue in verse 26: "And he that overcometh, and keepeth my works unto the end, to him will I give power over the nations." When God's people go to heaven, not all will be given the authority to rule. It will be given only to the overcomers.

Pillars in the Temple of God

The blessings of the overcomer do not end there. They continue in Revelation chapter three, where Jesus says,

> "He that overcometh, the same shall be clothed in white raiment; and I will not blot out his name out of the book of life, but I will confess his name before my Father, and before his angels"— Revelation 3:5.

Can you picture the scene? You are in the great halls of God. As you approach the very throne of the Almighty, Jesus says, "Look, Father, here he comes. He was faithful. He overcame against great odds." And you will find yourself standing in the presence of the Father and all the angels while Jesus tells how you overcame in your life. He is confessing you before His Father even as you confessed Him in your life. Hallelujah!

The blessings extend to our position in the throne room:

> "Him that overcometh will I make a pillar in the temple of my God, and he shall go no more out: and I will write upon him the name of my God, and the name of the city of my God"—Revelation 3:12.

What does He mean? Jesus is saying that if you are an overcomer, *you*—one of the living stones in His temple—will be a special stone, a monolith pillar.

I once visited the great temple of Karnak near Luxor in Egypt. This temple is the largest ever built, covering some three hundred acres. One of the amazing sights of the temple is a great hall with pillars thirty-six feet around. These huge pillars reveal the glory of the ancient Egyptian pharaohs.

Even in their decaying form they bear impressive witness to the greatness of those men.

Yet, God is building a temple far more magnificent than any built by man, and the overcomers will be His pillars. They will not have to come in and out before His face but can remain in His presence. If you are an overcomer, you will shine forth eternally with His glory upon you. Oh, how tremendous!

What Makes a Christian an Overcomer?

Jesus makes one final promise to the overcomer:

> "To him that overcometh will I grant to sit with me in my throne, even as I also overcame, and am set down with my Father in his throne"—Revelation 3:21.

How wonderful it will be to sit on the throne with Jesus, the great throne of all thrones! To have Jesus slide over and say to you, "Here, sit down with Me." You won't just sit there and keep the throne warm, but you will rule and reign in His kingdom and universe. Truly this is a greater privilege than anything our carnal mind could ever imagine.

All these blessings are for those who overcome. Oh, to be an overcomer, totally given over to God, "ruling my own spirit."

What separates the overcomers from other Christians? Are they stronger, more determined, or more spiritual? What makes a great Christian?

Every mighty man or woman of God passes through the fires of trial, trouble, and temptation. Because God loves us, He strives to make us lovely—at any cost. To do this He constantly burns away all human dross, refining His children to perfection. The prophet Malachi spoke of this process when he exclaimed of the Lord, "He is like a refiner's fire" (Malachi 3:2).

It's not the process, however, that separates the weak from the strong; it's learning to keep cool when the heat is on. It's coming out of the furnace with our fleshly weaknesses burned up. It's passing through the fires without being singed—with no lingering hurts, fears, grudges, or resentment—with not even the smell of smoke about us—just well-tempered love and faith in Jesus Christ.

CHAPTER ONE

Desperate for Change

Deep inside me there were words. They were alive, and they shook me to the core. God was saying, "Bob, you do not love them enough." What was to take place in the next ten minutes would dramatically transform my life.

Once I could have acknowledged what the Lord meant by not loving enough. In fact, I did not love at all. That was another time, another world, another man.

Hell in Our Home

I grew up in one of those nightmarish homes. As far back as I can remember there were no long periods of peace in my father's house. On three different occasions my parents' fighting resulted in bitter separations.

Although my father never finished the eighth grade, he had worked his way up the ladder in the postal department to become assistant director of foreign air mail for the whole country. Such a climb involved endless struggles at the office. With job competition and inter-office politics tearing him to shreds, the stress of his job took its toll at home.

If there was no smile on his face in the evening when he came from the subway and crossed the lot toward our apartment, I knew that within half an hour he most likely would be beating me with his belt. He usually vented his frustrations on my mother and me.

More vividly than my father's belt, I can remember my mother's seemingly constant criticism. Both my parents called me stupid, and I always felt inadequate. In their eyes it seemed I could do nothing right. Although they loved me and occasionally showed affection, those moments were so rare that they seemed almost a dream. As a youngster who didn't know any better, I considered this type of life normal. As a result an attitude of self-condemnation took root in my young life and thrived well into my adulthood.

Empty Religion?

My parents rarely went to church, yet they always sent me off to Sunday school. Despite my disinterest, they made sure I went through the church confirmation.

My religious upbringing seemed to be a waste of time since the church I attended taught nothing of Jesus' salvation or the real meaning of the cross. They preached moral and social issues. Those who were supposed to be watchmen for my soul were there simply to make the death process more comfortable. Looking back, I realize I was learning to fear God, twisted and mixed as it was with the fear of my father.

Although the rules at home seemed neither right nor just to me, I did have a moral upbringing. For this I praise God—that even through unbelieving parents He could reach my soul and lay a foundation that was to be the beginning of wisdom.

By high school I was sent off to a church-related military school where I was marched into the chapel every day and twice on Sundays. The droning sermons were meaningless to me; yet somehow the fear of God and the desire to do right were instilled in me. I decided to join the choir and sang for two years, acting as devout as possible on the outside, yet inwardly aware that something was wrong—I just didn't know what.

Turning My Back on God

One day, on my way back to school and dressed in uniform, I was waiting in a Chicago railway station. A young man sat down beside me and began to talk about Jesus. Had he asked me some religious or philosophical question I might have been interested, but I could not listen when he used the name "Jesus." Because it frightened and repulsed me, I turned him off. After all, I had religion. I had Jesus "in my own way," didn't I?

For three hours I sat there while he pleaded with me to receive Jesus Christ as my Savior. I nodded my head now and then saying, "Yes, I understand. But I am not that bad, you know. I even sing in the choir. I don't need that sort of thing." Still he begged me to give my heart to Christ.

Finally the call for my train came. I grabbed my bags and fled, but this persistent young man stayed right on my heels. Just before I jaunted through the gate, he stuffed some tracts and a card with his name and address into my hand.

"Think about what I've said," he begged. "Pray about it, give your life to Jesus, and write me about it. I'll be praying for you." I waved him off with "Sure, sure."

As I got on the train I breathed a sigh of relief. Slouching into a seat, I tried to wash from my mind all the words I had just heard. I wanted nothing to do with this "Jesus" he was talking about.

By the next day his name card had found its way into my wastebasket. But those tracts—they were something else. They were about a holy God. Yet a week later I finally discarded them, too. As they dropped into the trash, a barrier went up, separating me from God. From then on, God seemingly gave me over to the destructive consequences of my own life.

No Escape

I graduated from military academy and went on to Cornell University. This sudden burst of freedom after the restrictions of military school was too much for me to handle. I began living a wild, partying life, and eventually my grades plummeted. I was trying desperately to escape the darkness of my life, and movies were a convenient way to run from it all. Night after night, for months in a row, I went from one movie to another with an occasional party thrown in for variety.

The parties gradually grew in intensity, and I entered another phase in my downward slide into sin. I remember being sober only two nights during an intoxicated stretch that lasted three months. All my eating money went to buy cheap wine to help me escape.

But escape from what? I had come through a good high school; I was at a fine university; life should have been great. Instead, it was a nightmare. My grades dropped more sharply. I was destroying everything. Sin bred sin! Escape bred escape! Caught in a vicious downward spiral, I had no strength to extricate myself from the powerful grip of sin.

A History of Hatred

While at college, I met and married my wife. Our stormy engagement had been broken off six times. Neither of us was ready for marriage. Filled with problems and frustrations, we fought just as my parents and hers had done. The sins of the fathers were being visited upon the children. (See Exodus 20:5.)

I was finally forced to leave school because my grades were so low. Since the Korean War was still on, I was drafted within the month. In the Army my frustration and bitterness changed into utter hatred. Any moral fiber I had left was disintegrating, and I was becoming a hating animal. The hatred that had spawned in my father—and in his father before him—grew to full stature in me. I hated everyone: the sergeants, the officers, the WACS, my wife, and myself.

Soon my actions exposed my hatred. One day my one-year-old son committed an unforgivable sin by coming between me and my television set. As he began playing with the knobs, I became so enraged that I started beating him. My wife frantically began to hit me, screaming at me to stop.

I could no longer conceal the bitterness I felt. Finally one day my best friend, also an unbeliever, lamented, "Bob, you are so filled with hate that I just can't stand you anymore. I'm through." He walked out of my life, never to be my friend again.

Something broke inside me, and I wept a little as I watched him walk away. Only then did I realize that my life was a mess. At times, when I was alone, I even wept because of my helplessness to change. Realizing that God could not let me into heaven in my condition was a nightmarish thought. I knew I was destined for hell.

The Same Old Me

While in the Army I moonlighted as a bartender in the officer's club. Night after night I stole whiskey so my wife and I could get drunk. By now both of us were attempting to escape the pain of life.

Shortly before I was discharged, an old friend from Cornell University walked into the officers' club where I was working. Michael, a classmate, was now an officer while I was still a private. That night it hit me: I had only one life, and I was ruining it. At that moment I determined to straighten myself out.

The next day I applied to fourteen different universities, hoping to continue my education after my tour of duty. Only one accepted me, and then only on probation. I did not know it at the time, but God's hand was involved in my acceptance at the University of Kansas.

CHAPTER TWO

Something Is Missing

While studying geological engineering at the University of Kansas, I made every effort to change my life. I went back to church, hoping that regular attendance would help straighten me out. But half an hour after every service, I usually started the same old squabbling, bickering, and inevitable drinking.

Several times my wife and I threatened to separate. We couldn't stand each other, yet we couldn't bear to be apart. What a horrible pit life was.

Because I was attending church so faithfully, one morning the pastor asked, "Bob, how would you like to become Sunday school teacher of the seventh grade children?" I thought, That's it. That's what I need. Surely all Sunday school teachers go to heaven. Eagerly I accepted the books to study.

A Second Chance

The night before teaching my first Sunday school class, I was with a buddy in his machine shop on the campus. While he was working, I opened the Sunday school book to prepare for the next morning's lesson. As I stared down at the pages, my bewildered expression evidently signified something to Tom.

"Bob, what's the matter?"

"You know, I've got to be a Sunday school teacher in the morning, and I don't even know what to say to the kids."

"You really want to know?" Tom asked.

"Yeah."

"Well, let me show you." Tom reached up to his bookshelf and pulled down a book with a black cover. I had never noticed his Bible among all the engineering books. Although I had known him for several months, Tom had never said anything to me about church or religion or Jesus. I later discovered he had prayed earnestly since the day we met for an opportunity to share with me.

I quietly sat next to Tom as he opened his Bible. He began, "Bob, you know this Bible is the Word of God, don't you?" Yes, I remembered that from my early training. Then he asked, "So what you want to teach the kids tomorrow morning is not what some church says, nor what I say, but what God says, right?" I agreed.

"Let's look at God's general plan." He opened the Bible to Ezekiel 18:20 and read, "The soul that sinneth, it shall die." Then he turned to Romans 6:23, "The wages of sin is death."

He looked me right in the eye and said, "Bob, that means that if anyone sins, he deserves to die, not only physical death, but eternal death. He is unholy and cannot enter God's holy heaven. He is cut off forever."

Then Tom read me another passage. "There is none righteous, no not one. There is none that understandeth. There is none that seeketh after God. They are all gone out of the way" (Romans 3:10-12).

Tom quietly asked, "Bob, that means you deserve to die, too, doesn't it?"

I began to tremble. Once again I wanted to run, to hide, to turn off my ears. But I knew I couldn't; this time I had to face it. I was so desperate for an answer that I had to listen to God. Not able to speak, I merely nodded my head.

"But Bob, God does not want to send anyone to hell. He is a loving God, and He has given us one way out of this mess." This time I listened. Perhaps I had finally found the way.

Do You Want Jesus?

"Bob, do you know why Jesus died on the cross?"

"Well, I guess He wanted to be an example of being willing to die for what one believes in."

Tom agreed, but said it was more than that.

"Well," I ventured, "it showed that He would not fight back or hurt those who hurt Him."

Again Tom agreed, but said, "It's still more than that."

"I'm sorry, Tom. I just don't understand."

Tom explained very simply. "You see, Jesus is God Himself come in the flesh. When He died on that cross, Bob, He was paying the penalty for your sins. Jesus was your substitute. He took your punishment for you."

I could hardly believe my ears. Could this possibly be true? Tom handed me the Bible opened to John 3:16. I had never seen nor heard this passage! I had attempted to read the Scriptures several times before, but they meant nothing to me. I would usually bog down around the tenth or eleventh chapter of Genesis.

So for the first time I read, "For God so loved the world, that he gave his only begotten Son, that whosoever believeth in Him should not perish, but have everlasting life." When I started to hand it back, Tom suggested, "Read it again more slowly."

So I began again. When I reached "that whosoever believeth in Him," Tom stopped me. "Bob, does that say that whosoever loves his wife like he should, and treats his boy right, and lives a good moral life will not perish but have everlasting life?"

"No, it doesn't say that," I answered. "It just says whosoever believeth in Him."

"That's right. There are no strings attached; it is given to us as a gift. All we have to do is accept it and open our hearts to Jesus." Then he asked me, "Bob, do you want to receive forgiveness? Do you want Jesus in your heart?"

"Oh, yes, yes!" The words burst from my mouth. That night on the concrete floor of that little machine shop, Tom and I knelt and he led me in a sinner's prayer. "Oh, God, I'm ashamed. I've sinned against You and can't hide it anymore. I've hurt so many people; I've hated so much. Please forgive me. Jesus, come into my heart and take over my life. I've made a mess of it."

The man who cried out was a different Bob Heil from the one who had rejected God seven years before in the railway station. Back then I felt good enough, but now I saw myself as I really was—I had no excuses left. As I cried to God for forgiveness, I could actually feel the great weight of sin, like ten tons, being lifted from my shoulders. Tears flooded my eyes and poured down my cheeks as I asked the Lord Jesus to come into my heart and take over my life.

Tom said, "Look at Revelation 3:20. Jesus says, 'Behold, I stand at the door, and knock: if anyone hears my voice, and opens the door, I will come in to him and will sup with him, and he with me.' Did you open the door of your heart to Him?"

"Oh, yes!" I cried.

"Then where is He now according to His Word?"

"He is in my heart!" I burst out. I knew it was true. I could even feel His presence.

"Then know that you are truly forgiven and are a son of God."

Waves of joy and glory swept over me like the waves of the sea.

It's Real, Isn't It?

I jumped to my feet and pumped Tom's hand, "Thank you, Tom, thank you, thank you!" He showed me in the Scriptures that all who come to Jesus are truly forgiven and made children of God as simply as I was. What an exciting thought! This was the answer I had been searching for all my life.

"I've got to tell my wife!" I exclaimed. At two-thirty in the morning I ran the mile across campus, shouting to the heavens, "Thank You, God! Oh, thank You!"

I ran in the house, up the stairs, and into the bedroom. My wife was eight months pregnant with our second son and sound asleep. But I shook her awake and zealously asked, "Honey, honey, are you saved?"

I thought Tom and I were the only ones in the world who knew God's marvelous forgiveness. I tried to show her all the Bible passages Tom had shared with me.

"You mean anyone can go to heaven?" Letitia asked sleepily.

"Yes, if he truly repents."

"You mean someone like Adolf Hitler could go to heaven?"

"Well, if he had truly repented of all those sins, God would have forgiven him, too."

"Then I don't want to go to heaven if that's the kind of place it is," Letitia answered bluntly and fell back asleep.

She was not ready, and I had just turned her off. But over the next year she saw such an obvious change in my life that she, too, gradually gave in to God's more gentle pressure. Letitia yielded one facet of her life, but soon entire areas were surrendered to Jesus. Although her conversion was not as dramatic as mine had been, what a joyous day it was when she first confessed Christ.

During a Sunday afternoon drive, Letitia broke our mutual quietness by saying, "It's all real, isn't it?"

"What?" I asked, wondering what she was thinking about.

"Jesus has really paid for our sins." I cannot remember my answer except that I whooped and hollered for joy.

The Fiery Furnace

For a few months everything went fine; it was like having a honeymoon with the Lord. I thought all my problems were solved—all those years of religious teaching and an unhappy home life were seemingly erased. Just when I thought I had hurdled every obstacle, I awoke to the rude realization that the old pressures and defeats were still upon me.

I soon learned there was a very basic difference between the struggle I was now in and the one I had known before Christ saved me. Now it was not a nightmare—it was a *furnace*. I had entered into a holy furnace where God tests and proves the hearts of men. (See Psalm 66:10; Proverbs 17:3.)

The Lord describes our salvation in the following passage:

> For my name's sake will I defer mine anger, and for my praise will I refrain for thee, that I cut thee not off. Behold, I have refined thee, but not with silver; I have chosen thee in the furnace of affliction.
>
> For mine own sake, even for mine own sake, will I do it: for how should my name be polluted? and I will not give my glory unto another—Isaiah 48:9-11.

The Lord did not just want me saved, he wanted the pollution and evil out of my system. He wanted to make me into the image of God.

At first I was confused about the ways of God. Just as easily as He had saved me, I thought, He could instantly make me into a whole new person by merely speaking a word. But God showed me that the changes He wanted to make could only happen as I yielded my will and allowed Him to change me—a lifelong process.

Eventually I would discover what Job meant when he said, "For he knoweth the way that I take: when he hath tried me, I shall come forth as gold" (Job 23:10). If we can hold on and not faint from the heat in God's furnace of testing, we will come forth as pure gold.

> That the trial of your faith being much more precious than gold that perisheth, though it be tried with fire, might be found unto praise and honor and glory at the appearing of Jesus Christ—1 Peter 1:7.

Because our faith is much more precious to God than any gold, it must be purified to bring Him praise and honor. From the day we are saved until the day we go to glory, life is a joy. But it is also a fiery furnace used to melt us and mold us into

God's image. The furnace may be difficult, but it does not have to be a nightmare. And it is in the furnace that God makes overcomers.

A Miserable Christian

Billy Graham once said, "Some people have just enough Christianity to make them miserable." That was my experience. After the first invigorating rush of joy and excitement, I became a miserable Christian.

I had the joy of knowing I was Jesus' child, and the occasional touch of God on my life meant everything to me. But I still knew the agony of failure and sin. I had not been through the furnace yet. How sad that so many Christians today know only this same failure. They dodge their furnaces instead of enduring them God's way.

These first years of my Christian walk were not only miserable but exhausting. I sincerely wanted to work for God. Witnessing at every opportunity, I twisted conversations around to Jesus. I loved to back the other person into a corner—asking him if he was saved.

But my zeal for the Lord was intermingled with religious flesh. I later learned that a part of us wants to serve God in our own strength, our own way, our own willpower, our own resources, and for the purpose of earning God's favor. Doing the right thing in our own strength results in spiritual death.

This was one of the first things that God had to purge in His furnace. Religious flesh cannot please God, grow in God, or even do truly godly works. It may look holy on the surface, but not in the sight of God. My self-centered flesh just exhausted and frustrated me. It had to go.

Here Am I, Send Me

I can remember my calling into the ministry. While still a student at the University of Kansas, I searched for and found a Bible-teaching church. One Sunday a guest missionary from Nigeria shared how two native men had run several hundred miles to their mission headquarters in Obit Etom.

Exhausted but excited, these runners said, "We hear you have the true God in a book. Come and tell us about Him. We have built a house for the missionary to stay in. We are all waiting." The mission director scanned the roster of missionaries. One had twenty-three preaching stations, another had eighteen—everyone was overloaded. He had to answer, "Sorry, we have no one to send."

I could hardly believe my ears. My heart wrenched. They were begging for the true God.

The missionary continued, "In Japan, where many have heard our gospel broadcasts, we received 7,000 letters in one week begging us to send men to teach them of Christ and baptize believers. To all these letters we had to answer, 'Sorry, we have no one to send and no money to send them.' "

God's hand was on my heart. Despite being one month away from graduation and having three promising job offers in my field, I sensed God redirecting my steps. Right there in church I said, "I haven't got the money, but I'll go." Multitudes of people were begging for the truth. Someone had to tell them about Jesus.

That summer, instead of launching a successful career in geological engineering, I worked odd jobs until I started seminary in the fall. All I could think of was the mission field. In seminary I had mission posters on my wall, mission slogans on my desk, and maps of mission works on my doors.

When I finished school, I felt God was calling me to Nigeria. I was excited and expectant. I worried a little about the snakes but, praise God, I'd march right over them.

A Change in Plans

The seminary that was sending me, however, had just adopted a new policy—all candidates to the mission field must undergo psychiatric examination. There had been too many burn-outs on the mission field, and many missionaries had come back, suffering from culture shock.

As I was being examined by the seminary's local psychiatrist, I could tell that he did not know the Lord. The interview was going well when I saw an opportunity to witness. I began to share the story of my conversion, describing the great difference in my life before and after I received Jesus. The psychiatrist began writing furiously and with great agitation.

I was surprised to be sent to a second psychiatrist. After opening amenities, the first question out of his mouth was, "What did you tell that other psychiatrist?" Seeing another opportunity to witness, I reiterated my story. Again there was the same agitation on his face as he wrote furiously. When I was finished, he asked me no more questions. The interview was over.

The seminary wanted final confirmation of the psychiatrists' reports of my "instability," so this time they sent me to a psychologist who ran a battery of tests, pronounced me perfectly normal, and asked what I had told the psychiatrists. I took advantage of this third opportunity to testify for Christ.

This time, however, the psychologist was a born-again Christian and understood what I was saying. As my appointment concluded she said, "There is nothing wrong with you. I'll put in a good report, but it will not stand in the face of two psychiatrists. I'm only a psychologist.''

Within two weeks, however, God had turned my plans completely around. My call to Nigeria was gone, and I found myself as a pastor in a little parish in a small Missouri town.

For years I could not understand why it happened and wondered if I had missed the Lord. Eventually, I discovered that God had put me where He wanted me. In Missouri God helped me develop my talents and reach the fullness of my calling—a calling that has taken me to the jungles and squalor of the earth many times and is destined to take me there again. But the mission field was not to be my base.

God has a perfect plan for every believer's life. If we truly seek to serve Him and remain a yielded vessel, God will keep us in the center of His will. All we have to do is trust Him.

Is This All There Is?

The passion to reach the lost multitudes still burned within me. Although I was a pastor of a local church, I kept thinking beyond my congregation. Soon I had a radio program and weekly newspaper column that preached Christ crucified. I performed many "admirable" deeds, but elements of my ministry were not led by the Spirit— they were simply works of religious flesh.

I preached my heart out to people who always responded, "Fine sermon, Pastor," but as the months turned into years, I saw no change in their lives. My preaching was not totally in vain—a little growth here and there was evident—but much of my effort seemed to be wasted.

I read the exciting accounts of multitudes that were dramatically healed and converted under the preaching of Stephen, Philip, and the early apostles. My ministry seemed so far from that; I knew I was only spinning my wheels.

My second congregation in another part of the state was larger, but most of my energy was spent just keeping the committees and boards of the church together. Very little true spiritual work was being accomplished.

With deepening frustration I found myself just following the same routine year after year after year. I pleaded with God, "Is this what life is about? Is this the meaning of ministry—to go on with the same program for forty years?" My frustration became an agony.

I began to loathe the inexcusable religious flesh that was exhibited by my congregation and me. We had a form of godliness but no power. We were far from being the overcomers Jesus described in Revelation 2 and 3.

I began to plead with God to change my life. In desperation I cried, "Fill me with Your Spirit, take over my entire life, give me a ministry with power." Little did I realize what I was asking for.

CHAPTER THREE

Please Pray for Me

One day as I sat in my study, I received a visit from a man in my congregation.

"Pastor," he began, "something in James chapter five has me puzzled."

"What is it?" I asked.

"Well, it says if anyone is sick he should call for the elders of the church to pray for him and anoint him with oil in the name of the Lord, and the Lord will raise him up."

"Yes, that is right," I replied. "We pray for the sick."

"But," he argued, "the Bible says they will get better."

I sidestepped his point by saying, "Well, *when* they get better, it is the *Lord* who makes them better."

His expression revealed that he was not completely satisfied with my answer, but he didn't raise any more questions about the issue. I was glad because healing was a rather ticklish subject.

About a week later my parish worker came to see me. "I've got a question, Pastor," she said, "about a passage in James five. Scripture says if anyone is sick, he should call for the elders of the church to anoint him with oil and pray for him, and the Lord will raise him up."

"We do pray for the sick," I informed her.

"Yes, but the Bible says they will get better."

Those same words! At the time I didn't realize the Lord was trying to say something to me.

"Well, when they get better it is the Lord who makes them better." She gave me that same unsatisfied look. Then she asked, "Well, what do you think about this anointing with oil?"

"Susan, that was just an old custom in those days. We don't do that now because it does not really amount to anything."

She left, and again I forgot the subject—until about a week later when Linn Haitz, my assistant pastor, came to see me.

Coincidence or Conspiracy?

Linn was a dear missionary friend who had come to stay with our family after being denied a visa to re-enter Nigeria. Because he had written a book exposing the witchcraft practices in that country, the government had refused to permit him to return. Now serving as assistant pastor, Linn often had spiritual insight into areas that I found confusing.

As he took a seat across from my desk, Linn asked, "Bob, what do you make of this passage in James five?" and he repeated the same verse.

"What is this—a conspiracy?" I demanded.

"What do you mean?"

I told him of Susan's and Dale's visits with the same question. "Well, I don't know anything about them," he replied, "But what do you make of the passage?"

So I gave him the same answer. "We do pray for the sick."

"Yes, but the Bible says they will get better!"

Still it did not dawn on me. I sidestepped the issue again. "Well, when they get better, it is the Lord who makes them better."

Linn was not satisfied by my weak answer. "But, Bob, it doesn't say 'when' or 'if' or 'they might' get better; it is a promise just like the gospel."

I was stunned. "My, you're right." I admitted.

Linn then asked, "What do you think about this anointing with oil?"

"Linn, that was just an old custom that doesn't pertain to today," I answered.

"But are you sure? Scripture doesn't say it was just a custom for then."

I decided I needed to study this subject before anyone else came with the same question. I began to pour over the Scriptures, and within a few hours found promise after promise pertaining not only to spiritual needs, but earthly needs as well. I discovered that the Father sent Jesus to the cross not just for my soul, but for my body, my life, my finances—my total being. His shed blood provides redemption for every facet of life.

Despite seeing these truths in Scripture in a matter of hours, I studied them for months until they overwhelmed the fear inside me about stepping into untested waters. I discovered a great difference between seeing the truth and believing the truth.

Finally my fear melted before the Word and turned to joy! What an exciting discovery! Little did I know God was about to give it special meaning for me.

The Right Moment

I had suffered from back trouble for years. When we were in seminary, Letitia and I had taken judo lessons. One night as we practiced on a mattress in the living room, I landed wrong.

Although I did not realize it at the time, I had ruptured the bottom disc in my back. My back grew progressively stiffer and more painful with each passing day. In class I had to lie down on the floor because I could not stand the hard wooden seats. I worked as a draftsman to put myself through seminary, but could not tolerate the backless drafting stools for more than twenty minutes. Eventually I was forced to retreat to the floor in the back of the drafting room for relief.

Realizing I could not spend the rest of my life lying on the floor, I went to the doctor. The next thing I knew I was undergoing surgery. The ruptured disc was removed by a new technique that put me back on the job in five days.

Just a year later the wife of one of the professors had this same operation, but she was left paralyzed from the waist down. Eventually she died from the complications. That scared me. I began to be more careful about my back—how I slept, sat, and lifted things. The doctors warned me that the next disc up could rupture at any time because of its weakened condition.

Time had passed without complications. Now, years later, I was studying these Scripture passages on healing.

Then it happened. One morning I was shaving when suddenly a sharp pain knifed the weakened disc. I was rigid with pain. Within a week I had resorted to lying on the floor again to alleviate the pain. I was helplessly stretched out when Linn Haitz came into the room.

Because Linn lived with my family, he had seen me lying on the floor many times during that week, but he had said nothing. This time I asked, "Linn, would you pray with me about my back?"

"Bob, I've been waiting for you to ask me," he eagerly responded. Once again I had met a man who prayed and waited for the right moment.

From Believer to Receiver

"I even bought a bottle of olive oil," I told him, "because I want to do it just like James five says."

I knelt down with my hand on the Bible open to the passage in James. As I prayed, I spelled out every truth I had learned in those months of studying healing. "Lord, You healed everyone who came to You, You never change, and You are no respecter of persons. You died for my back as well as my spirit. I know Your atonement was for the whole person. I know I am not worthy, but I know I am a child of God forgiven of my sins because You died for me on the cross. Therefore, I now ask You to heal me."

Then Linn made the sign of the cross with the oil on my forehead, laid his hands on me, and began to pray. As he prayed, a sensation slowly traveled down my back until it came to the vertebrae where the disc was out. Suddenly my back jumped as if the knife were yanked out, and within two seconds the pain and soreness had melted away.

I jumped to my feet and began dancing around the living room shouting, "I'm healed! I'm healed! Thank You, God, thank You, thank You!" What joy! I certainly wasn't acting like a Lutheran pastor, but I couldn't stop rejoicing. What a victory!

That night I put my healing to the test. I slept on my left side, the side I hadn't been able to sleep on for years. There was not a bit of pain. I tried the next night and the next. I was like a new man. The Bible was true. It was real. Oh, what a wonderful God!

CHAPTER FOUR

I Want It All

Can you imagine how this healing experience changed my ministry? Immediately the New Testament came alive with meaning. Healing was for now—for God's people today!

I fervently reread the New Testament with new eyes and a new heart that asked, "Lord, where is the overcoming power those early Christians had? Why can't we walk in such supernatural ways? Where are the miracles?"

Daily, almost hourly, my heart cried out to God as I searched the New Testament like never before. God promises, "You will seek Me and find Me, when you search for Me with all your heart" (Jeremiah 29:13, NKJV).

I found the answer in the book of Acts. Concerning Pentecost, Jesus said, "Ye shall receive *power,* after that the Holy Ghost is come upon you" (Acts 1:8, italics added).

There were two major questions in my mind. First, was the Holy Spirit received when God's people were saved or baptized in water, or was this a separate dimension of blessing? Second, are the gifts of the Holy Spirit still being offered today?

Studying the experience at Pentecost, I discovered no mention of water baptism. This blessing had been poured out on those who were already believers. The baptism of the Holy Spirit was a different experience altogether. I also read that Philip ministered to Samaritans who were already baptized, *believing Christians.* They were rejoicing in the Lord, but they had not yet received the Holy Spirit. (See Acts 8:15,16.) They were *born* of the Spirit, but not yet *baptized* in the Spirit. Indeed, it was a *separate* dimension.

Still I questioned, "Is it for now?" Then I read the great sermon Peter preached on the day of Pentecost in which he quoted the prophet Joel: "And it shall come to pass in the last days, saith God, I will pour out my Spirit upon all flesh" (Acts 2:17). I thought, If they were in the last days then, what are we in today?

The passage that fully convinced me was 1 Corinthians 13:8-12, which describes the supernatural gifts that come with the baptism of the Holy Spirit. Speaking in tongues, prophecy, and the word of knowledge are described as being imperfect and being only in part. When will these imperfect things pass away? "But when that which is perfect is come, then that which is in part shall be done away'' (1 Corinthians 13:10).

The text went on to describe when the perfect was coming. It was not describing the time when the written Scriptures were available to the church, as I had been taught. Instead it said very simply the perfect would come when we see Jesus ''face to face,'' when we know Him as He knows us. That has not happened, so the perfect is not yet here. Therefore the things ''that are in part'' are still available. They are for today!

Give Me Everything!

I began to hunger and thirst for those blessings. I wanted everything God had for me. I didn't want to miss a single blessing. I knew I had only one life and that my time on earth was not just a practice run. This was it! I knew I needed all the help I could get.

I talked to Linn and discovered that he was already baptized with the Holy Spirit. No wonder he had experienced so many miracles in his own ministry! I wanted that same power.

I also wanted others to know it was available. I had to share this news with my congregation. Teaching these neglected blessings would put an end to the lethargy and the apathy in the church, I thought. This deficit of power was the reason

the church was being turned upside down by the
world instead of the church turning the world
upside down as it had done in that first century.
I enthusiastically preached these truths.

This was a great time of learning for me. New
revelations seemed to continually pour into me—
truths about fasting, the demon world, and watchings in the night. Healings and miracles and all
sorts of new experiences opened up to me. Concepts of the Body of Christ began to take shape,
and I began to see God's plan more completely.

Linn and I heard of seven other pastors in our
denomination who had received the baptism in
the Holy Spirit. We wrote to them asking if they
would like to attend a conference at our church,
which was located near the center of the country.

Immediately the answers came back: "Yes, it's
a great idea! Did you invite so and so . . . ?" After
collecting forty-four names of pastors in our
denomination who had already received this blessing, we wrote to invite all of them. Despite their
initial enthusiasm, however, only twelve pastors
along with some of their wives and laymen could
attend our conference.

This small conference was intended to be a private study on the separate experience of the Holy
Spirit. I wanted more confirmation that I was on
the right track, but I did not really want my congregation to know what we were discussing. Most

of all, I personally hoped to receive the baptism in the Holy Spirit that weekend.

Wanting to prepare myself to receive the full impact of this great blessing, I had fasted for twelve days in three-day stretches to be more open to God.

My Moment of Truth

After the morning session on the first day of the conference, we all went up to the altar to pray. There for the first time I heard some of the other people praying in tongues. The sound of these strange languages was a little frightening, but I didn't want to judge it. Then one of the pastors turned around and asked the handful of us who were seated in the pews, "Is there anyone here who wants to receive the baptism in the Holy Spirit?"

I turned to Letitia and put my hand on her shoulder. Because I believed that she thought all of this was crazy, I gave her a little sermon as I started to get up. "Honey, there's the invitation. I've got to go. I know it's a blessing from God for all His people, and I want every blessing I can get my hands on." Years later my wife told me that she was trying to get up to run forward, but my hand was holding her down!

With that I arose and knelt at the first steps that led up into the chancel. I should have walked all

the way up to the altar rail so that I could have
something to lean upon, but my false humility kept
me kneeling at the entrance way to the chancel.

All twelve pastors gathered around to lay their
hands on me. Some prayed in English, and some
prayed in tongues. Boy, they are really giving me
the works, I thought. Some prayed softly, and
some prayed loudly.

I lifted up my hands and cried, "Lord, fill me
with Your Spirit, fill me to the brim, pressed down,
shaken together, and running over."

Nothing happened. Nothing that I could tell,
anyway. Again I asked the Lord. Again, there was
nothing. Again and again I asked. The men sought
the Lord for me, but without result. I opened my
mouth to let the words come out. I waited—
nothing came. As the minutes dragged by (about
ten minutes in all), I agonized more and more and
became very discouraged. I tried so hard to pray
in tongues, but nothing would come.

Feelings or Faith?

Finally, in despair and not knowing what else
to do, I got up and walked down the aisle of the
church. I wanted to run. I was the host pastor, and
yet nothing had happened. Pastor Dave Dorpat
from Nebraska followed me out. As we sat down
together on the front steps, he asked, "Bob, you

didn't feel anything, did you?'' I shook my head. He said, "But you received the baptism in the Holy Spirit, so thank God for it.''

"But nothing happened.''

"Oh, Bob, you are trying to take it by feelings instead of by faith,'' Dave countered. "Faith in the Scriptures—that is where you have to stand. Don't the Scriptures say, 'If we being evil know how to give good gifts to our children, how much more *shall* our Heavenly Father give the Holy Spirit to those who ask Him?' ''

"Yes,'' I nodded my intellectual assent.

"Then God kept His side of it. You have it, so thank Him for it.''

"But nothing happened,'' I lamented.

"Bob, stop looking at 'happenings' and stand on the Bible,'' Dave insisted. "Does Scripture say if two of you agree on earth regarding anything I will grant the request?''

"Yes, it says that.''

"Were the men who prayed for you agreed that you should receive the baptism of the Spirit?''

"Yes,'' I said sheepishly.

"Were you agreed to it?''

"Why, yes.''

"Then you have received it; thank Him for it.''

"Okay. Thank You, God,'' I began haltingly.

He nudged me, "Thank Him for the Holy Spirit.''

"Thank You, God, for baptizing me in the Holy Spirit. Thank You. Praise the Lord."

I didn't pray in tongues, but I began to feel something inside. The only way I can describe it is "faith." I began to feel faith rising. I knew I received what I had asked for. Now I thanked the Lord in earnest. I could have prayed in tongues right then and there, but I didn't know how. But, boy, was I happy! Down deep inside I knew that the Lord had touched me and that I now had it. I wish I had been able to stand on sheer faith, but now the faith and the feelings were both there.

A New Day Dawns

I practically floated back inside the church and exuberantly declared to the other pastors, "Don't worry about me if I didn't pray in tongues. I have the baptism; the Lord just quickened it to my heart." Then I witnessed another amazing thing. I heard them all cry out with a loud voice, "Praise the Lord!" (something I had never heard our denominational pastors do before). A new day was dawning in my life.

Ten minutes after I had asked for prayer, my wife came forward and the men laid hands on her. Feeling something rising inside her, my wife covered her mouth, ran home to the parsonage, and locked the front door behind her. After running into the bedroom and locking that door, she said, "All right, Lord." She began to sing in tongues. Mind you, my wife is not a musician. She can't sing in English to this day, but she sings beautifully in tongues!

That afternoon we stood in a prayer circle, holding hands and praying one after another. As one man prayed, he stopped suddenly and began to utter prophecy. I had never heard prophecy before, but as it came, courses of electricity shot through my body. I discovered later that no one else had felt it, but I knew it was God. He was saying, "I have started a new work. I will build it, and I will make it a pillar in My temple." How thrilled I was! I was bubbling and beaming with joy, but still there had been no tongues.

The Least Gift?

That night, while I was sound asleep, the Lord came into my room about two o'clock. Again I sensed wave after wave of electricity coursing through me. I awoke and could hardly breathe. I knew the Lord was standing there. I could not hear or see Him, but I knew He was there and that He wanted me to pray. I went into our darkened living room and began to pray. I tried desperately to pray in tongues.

There had been a day when I had despised tongues. Thinking it was the kookiest thing I had ever heard, I had prayed, "God, give me the Holy Spirit, but not tongues." Now God was reminding me of that past prayer, and His response brought sudden conviction.

"Who are you to despise My gift?"

"Oh, Lord, I am sorry, but it is the least of all Your gifts," I stammered.

"Who told you it is the least of My gifts? The Scriptures do not say that. Besides, who are you that you think you deserve more than just the least of My gifts?" I repented that instant.

Now I was asking God to give me the gift of tongues. I didn't want to miss any of God's blessings.

I knelt there in the dark crying out to God for the gift. I pointed to my mouth saying, "Ah, ah." But nothing came. Finally I said, "All right, God, then help me to pray in English. Guide my thoughts and help me to pour my heart out to You, for I must pray." Suddenly my mind welled forth with thoughts, and I poured them out to God.

For almost two hours I was there on my knees in the living room. The prayer was in English, but now the Lord guided the thoughts! My prayer was never repetitious, never humdrum. What a blessing! Communion with God was suddenly rich and alive.

I could have prayed in tongues then, or in any of the weeks and months that followed, but I didn't know how. I strained and strained to hear words in my head, but I could hear nothing. Later I learned God doesn't put the words in our head.

Then I thought that He would grab my lips and tongue and move them all around to make the right sounds since I didn't know what the right sounds were. But God doesn't put the gift in our mouth or our throat. He puts the gift in our heart. As Jesus said, "For out of the abundance of the heart the mouth speaks" (Matthew 12:34, NKJV).

I Give Up

Finally after four months of desperation I cried, "God, I give up. I just give up; I can't wait any longer. I will just make sounds to You. I will dedicate the sounds, and You will have to put them together. I don't know how, but I've got to do something." I realized anything officially dedicated to the Lord would come under His reigning power. (See Romans 6:16.)

Beginning to make sounds, I spoke about two sentences and stopped. "No, that was only me," I concluded. I still doubted that what I'd dedicated to God was under His control. Because I was looking for feelings instead of standing by faith, I didn't try again for several weeks.

Of course I was making the sounds, but I hadn't prayed enough to have anything spiritual going on in my soul. After having spoken only a few sentences of simple sounds—like baby talk in a new language—I had felt nothing. It felt so natural as though it was just me. I didn't realize that I was supposed to do the praying and God was supposed to do the listening—the same way I communicated with Him in English.

Isn't the Holy Spirit supposed to guide the sounds? Yes, but He does it very naturally. He wants to guide our prayers even when we pray in English.

Again I hungered for the blessing. I yearned to pray in tongues because I wanted every bit of edification I could get my hands on. Once again I decided to pray sounds to God, hoping that He would shape them into words and sentences. I dedicated all sounds and letters to Him and began making utterances that were perhaps a few paragraphs in length. Then I stopped. "Was that me or not?" I questioned.

I still *felt* nothing happening in my spirit. I wasn't trusting my prayers of dedication, so for several more weeks I said nothing else in tongues.

Until the Gift Excels

I decided to attend a regional convention of the Full Gospel Business Men's Fellowship. The morning sermon thrilled my spirit. During the prayer time afterward, I again dedicated myself to Jesus.

"Lord, I'm going to just pray sounds to You. I don't know whether they're right or wrong. But, I dedicate them to You and if some of them are right, put life into them. If some are wrong, melt them away. If there is any sound or syllable or letter of some alphabet that is part of my prayer language but I'm not using it, let me realize that sound or letter and I'll dedicate it to You.

"I'll start using it and working at the gift until it excels. You must put it together because I don't know what else to do. And Lord, I'm going to do it for five minutes to give You enough time to do something."

I'm glad I said that. In the months of waiting I had seen in Scripture where a person is allowed to work at the gifts until he excels. (See 1 Corinthians 14:12.) I decided to work at praying in tongues, trusting God to put it together.

I started with some "S's" because I knew that every language probably had an "S" in it. I added some "E's" and "M's." Because my speech was very mechanical, discouragement hounded me. But I determined to press on.

After two minutes of saying the same sounds over and over again, I realized that I wasn't using any "F's." Most languages have an "F" in them, I thought to myself, and if this is supposed to be a language and not just gibberish, then most likely it ought to have an "F."

"Lord, I dedicate 'F's' to You. If You don't want them, throw them away." I started to use "F's" with the few sounds that I had. When my prayer language began to flow a little better, I stopped and thought about it some more. I'm not using any "L's," I thought. Every language I know anything about has an "L" in it.

"Lord, I dedicate 'L's' to You. Again, if You don't want them, just melt them away." So I started using "L's," and it began to flow even better. I was getting rather happy about it and paused again. Maybe my language has a guttural sound like a German "ach," I thought. Tongues don't have to sound like English. When I dedicated that to the Lord my tongue continued to flow.

Cultivating a Prayer Language

Over the next two weeks, I rededicated myself two or three times a day and began praying in tongues, each time adding a little more. Some syllables didn't seem to fit, but most did. As my tongue began to flow more beautifully, the feelings I had been looking for began to come. I sensed more and more of a breakthrough. My heart began to rise like a rocket off the launching pad. I grew bolder, and my praise ascended with great power to God.

Since then praying in tongues has been sweet and beautiful. I finally realized that my prayer language had been there all along—just waiting for me to use it. Just as I prayed in English, I was to do the praying in tongues. God had not put it in my mind or my throat. He had put it in my spirit.

Not only that, but I could use it whenever I wanted whether I felt spiritually "up" or not. God does not rescind His promises or gifts. Scripture says, "For the gifts and calling of God are without repentance" (Romans 11:29).

If you have ever experienced tongues, you've still got them. Just dedicate yourself and whatever results to God, open your heart and your mouth, and pray to God in sounds. You can start with any sound. God will pick it up wherever you start.

You are not pushing the Holy Spirit around by working at the gift. You are simply allowing yourself to be an open vessel for the Spirit to use. Leave the results and any correction up to Him. If it takes weeks, keep working at it—cultivating a prayer language is worth the effort!

CHAPTER FIVE

In Step With Jesus

I had wanted to keep our little pastors' conference a secret from my congregation. But the men in attendance had to be housed and, of course, they had to be fed. While we were holding our meetings at one end of the basement, the ladies who were preparing the food were setting up tables at the other end.

Hearing bits and pieces of a very animated discussion across the room, one of these women became overwhelmed by curiosity. "Come over here and listen to this!" she whispered to the others. Before we knew it, a little circle of chairs formed around the pastors. These women called their husbands at work and said, "Don't go home to eat; come right over to the church. You've got to hear what these men are saying!"

During that two and a half day conference, twelve people from my congregation received the infilling of the Spirit. We began to realize that our prayer life and our Bible study life had been greatly enhanced by our new experience. God's joy and anointing rested upon us. Some people in our group had visions; some spoke in tongues; some sang in tongues; and some prophesied. Miraculous healings began to happen.

Surely we are overcomers now, I thought. Little did I know how much we had to learn.

Praying for Open Doors

Those of us who had been baptized in the Spirit prayed earnestly that God would show us the next step. We felt compelled to share these blessings with the others in the congregation, but how would we go about it?

The Lord spoke within me and said, "I want you to walk with Me. I do not want you to walk ahead of Me like Jacob who put goat's hair on the back of his hands and neck, trying to force the blessing. (See Genesis 27:6-17.) Nor do I want you to lag behind Me, for these are blessings that My people need. They must not be hidden."

"But Lord, how do we do that?"

Many of us either do not speak at all about Spirit baptism because we are afraid, or we speak too much and try to kick the doors open. God wants us to pray them open even as the apostle Paul advised the Colossians, "Meanwhile, praying also for us, that God would open to us a door for the word" (Colossians 4:3, NKJV).

The Lord showed us three things we had to do if we wanted to walk with Him.

First, we had to pray earnestly for the open doors of opportunity. We weren't to collar our brothers and sisters and force them to listen. We weren't to kick the doors open; we were to pray them open.

Second, we were to watch closely and carefully for the doors to open. We were to have an excited eagerness in our heart to see the opportunities that the Holy Spirit would set up. We needed to stay alert and in a state of expectancy to find a person with whom we could share the blessing.

Third, when the Spirit opened their hearts to listen, we needed to speak only what the Spirit gave. We were not to add more to it; just answer their questions. He would use the answer to put a hunger in their hearts to ask another question or to seek more.

This simple three-step plan was all that God needed to start His work. We began to pray for open doors. We pushed no one. We didn't beat anyone over the head with the truth. We just prayed for God to touch hearts and to help us to see when the time was right. We did not kick any doors open; we prayed them open. We let the Lord woo them in as we loved them. Within the next year, fifty to sixty people in our congregation received the baptism of the Spirit.

Ready to Receive

As more people in our congregation experienced the infilling of the Holy Spirit, the word got around quickly, and tension began to build in the hearts of some parishioners. I had started two Bible classes for studying the Holy Spirit, one on Wednesday night and one on Thursday morning. In addition, I had distributed lists of Bible passages for all the families in the church to study.

Finally, after that first year I knew that those in the Bible courses must sooner or later be asked to make a decision on receiving the baptism in the Holy Spirit. John Sherril, in his classic book, *They Speak With Other Tongues,* calls this decision stepping through "the little red door."

For a year many of our members had felt that these teachings were very interesting and even fascinating. They had asked many good, honest, biblical questions, and they had grown. Now they needed to step across the threshold.

Seeing that many more were ready for the infilling with the Holy Spirit, we held a special Wednesday night service for all who were interested. Rodney Lensch, a very dynamic servant of God, was our speaker that night, and twelve more people in our congregation received the baptism with the Spirit.

What's Happening at the Church?

During the service that night, some people prayed aloud in tongues. One lady became highly incensed and stormed out. As she returned home, her husband was just arriving from his job. She told him all the "horrible" things that were happening. He became very upset and called the church.

Susan, our parish worker, who by that time had also been filled with the Spirit, went over to their house to explain the Scriptures. After three hours of showing them that this experience was scriptural and for today, they were much more calm and at peace.

When the husband told his co-workers what had happened, however, they began to ask him questions that he could not answer. By the end of the next day he was not the only one who was confused and newly angered—so were those who were talking to him!

Within a few days a great furor raged in our church. A massive wall seemed to suddenly divide our congregation. This wall was made up of huge stones—stones of pride ("Are you trying to say I don't have *everything*?") and stones of jealousy ("Are you saying you are better than I am? Are you trying to say my grandfather and my father before me were not Christians?").

Of course we answered all these questions. We explained that we were not claiming to be better than anyone. But we could say we *ourselves* were better than we used to be. We pointed out how these blessings are for everybody, for strong and weak Christians alike. They are gifts that come by grace—no one has earned them.

Shaking the Foundations

The biggest stones in the wall were fears— especially the fear of the unknown and the fear of men. If you have never been in an airplane, you are likely to be afraid the first time you fly. Some who have flown many times are still afraid.

Christians fear how their friends will react if they receive the baptism in the Holy Spirit. Others are overly conscious of what people think about them. In fact, some people are disturbed if only one person thinks badly of them. Such fear is a powerful and destructive force.

Perhaps the greatest fear of all is the fear of getting closer to God. I believe we all naturally fear that the darkness within us will be exposed if we get closer to God.

This fear exists because our foundations are built to some extent on the wrong things. Sometimes only part of our foundation is built on Jesus Christ, while the other part is built on the church and its tradition. Then right as the church may be, right as those traditions may be, in those areas our foundation is built on Christ only in a secondary way. If change threatens the traditions even a little, such as using guitars in the services, it shakes people up.

None of us has his foundation entirely in Jesus Christ. Part of our security comes from other sources, and so our lives get shaken occasionally by Jesus until those other foundations crumble. He is a jealous Lord who wants His bride to be built on Him alone. We fear having our other foundations exposed.

Gripped by Fear

A great servant of God who often worshiped the Lord was praying in the temple one day, and he saw God high and lifted up. About Him were six seraphim, each with six wings. One cried to the other, "Holy, holy, holy is the Lord of hosts. The whole earth is full of His glory."

What did this man of God say? Did he say, "Oh, how great to be this close to You, O God! How wonderful it is to see Your glory"? No, he said, "Woe is me! for I am undone; because I am a man of unclean lips."

This fear-gripped man was the prophet Isaiah. Because he saw the sinful areas of his life in light of God's holiness, the Lord had to send an angel to reassure him that his sins were forgiven. (See Isaiah 6:1-7.)

I read about a man who was the same way. During the early outpouring of the Holy Spirit, this old man was quite well respected throughout the Christian community. One day as he prayed, he heard a voice behind him like the sound of many waters and thunders. He turned and saw his old friend Jesus—the One with whom he had been so close.

The Christ he saw this time was different than he had ever known Him. His hair was shining white. His eyes blazed like fire, and His feet were like burnished brass in the furnace. When he saw Jesus in His glory, he fell down in utter fear at His feet as a dead man. What did Jesus have to say to that fine old charismatic? He said, "Fear not, John," and raised him up with a comforting word that took away the fear. (See Revelation 1.)

If Isaiah and the apostle John were afraid of getting closer to God and having a deeper experience with Him, then who was I to condemn those in the congregation who were afraid of the same thing? Because of fear they fought against the unknown. How could I fault them?

When we are afraid of something, we want to stay far from it. If you are afraid of snakes, you may never visit the reptile house at the zoo. If you are afraid of flying, you won't go near a plane. You will take Amtrak or drive your car, even if it is a great inconvenience.

What if we cannot get away from our fears? What if the object of our fears sits in the pew in front of us or in the pew across the aisle? Then we cannot stay away from it. What do we then do? We try to drive the fear away. At such a moment, we do not use logic or rational thinking—we act on feelings alone.

Fear is a rotten, gut-deep feeling. As this fear gripped many in our congregation, our testing fire got hotter.

CHAPTER SIX

Whose Problem Is It?

We did not realize it at the time, but our group of Spirit-filled believers was finally in the place where God could begin to fashion us into overcomers. The furnace became more and more uncomfortable to the point of being almost unbearable.

Oh, the terrible gossip that was going around! Stories were twisted out of shape, and lies were spawned from the very pit of hell. By the time the stories got to me they were fifth hand and very ugly. I became extremely disturbed and burdened, especially since I could not put a finger on those at fault. Who was saying what to whom? No one would confess, and no one dared to face us directly.

Give Me the Problem

At last in desperation, in the very heat of the furnace, I went to the Lord in my office one night and lamented, "Oh, Lord, how do I cope with this malicious talk? I don't know who has been saying what to whom. Lord, how do I handle this? How do I stop it?"

Again the Lord spoke deep within me as He had done several times before. His words are filled not only with wisdom, but with life itself. His words give the answer and bring glorious freedom. God said, "My son, why don't you hand the problem to Me?"

I quickly answered, "All right, Lord, take it, take it, but what am I supposed to do?"

"I thought you just gave the problem to Me."

"I did, I did. But what am I supposed to do? What am I supposed to say?"

"If you have given the problem to Me, then you need not do anything except what I lay in front of you to do. The problem is Mine. When you give Me a problem, do not just hand it to Me, but also hand Me the *responsibility* that goes with it."

That was the key word—responsibility. How many times I had handed the Lord a problem only to repeatedly worry about it as though things were still up to me! How those concerns had churned in my mind and robbed me of peace!

Rolling Off My Burdens

At length the Lord was able to reveal to me how I was to hand Him this problem. The Scriptures say, "Commit thy way unto the Lord; trust also in him; and he shall bring it to pass" (Psalm 37:5). As I studied that verse, I looked up *galal,* the Hebrew word for commit. This unusual word means to "roll off onto."

I thought back to my seminary days when I was moonlighting on a job that required me to unload one hundred pound sacks of flour from a railroad car into the back of a bakery. The sacks on top were too high to drop down on the dolly, so we had to carry some of them on our backs.

If you have a one hundred pound sack on your back, you do not try to set it down by leaning backward until it touches the ground. The way we solved the problem was to roll the heavy sack onto a metal-topped table by the door. Then we could slide it wherever we wanted.

This is what the Lord was saying in the Scriptures. Do you feel broken or crushed beneath a heavy problem? God says to roll it off—roll it right onto His shoulders.

The Lord did not say to roll only the very heavy burdens onto Him. Notice that He said, "Commit thy way unto me." The "way" in the Hebrew means the whole life—every step, every detail of life, and every problem. Give everything to Jesus.

Suppose only an hour before dinner your husband tells you that the boss is coming over and bringing his wife. Your hair is a mess, it's your turn to pick up the children after school, you haven't a thing to cook, and the house is a shambles! Give it to Jesus. Hand it to Him and let Him have the situation. The evening will be a success and your preparation will be much more meaningful and peaceful.

If you cannot find the car keys, give that to Jesus, too. In a sense, you let Him do all the fussing and stewing. You know what? You'll find your keys a lot faster, and you'll feel a lot better about it. Jesus will take everything you hand Him—everything.

Whom Do You Trust?

The verse in Psalm 37 says not only to "commit thy way unto the Lord," but also to "trust in him." Picture a depositor patronizing his bank. Would he be nervous, upset, and afraid to give the teller his money? Would he hand her his deposit slip, closely watch her count the money, and wonder what is going to happen to his hard earned cash when she places it in a drawer? Out of nervousness, would he get back in line a second time and ask if he can see his money? If he did such a thing, the bank might tell him to either trust them or take his business elsewhere.

Of course, most of us do not do that. We walk into the bank very casually, reach into our pocket or purse, and hand the teller the money. We might not even bother to check our duplicate slip. Afterward we drive off without a second thought. We trust the bank.

If we can trust them with a big item like *money,* then we can trust God with anything. He does not make mistakes, and He does not embezzle. Once you have given a problem to Him, there is no error from that point on. That entire situation now belongs to Him.

I know a man who gave God his business only to have it plunge toward bankruptcy until he was forced to sell. This man was puzzled and confused for a while, until another opportunity suddenly opened up. Jesus did not really want him in that business in the first place. Out of the ashes of failure, the Lord went on to build success.

I finally handed Jesus all the gossip, saying, "Take it, Lord, it's Yours. I don't care any more about who is saying what. If people give me funny looks on the street, I'm just going to ignore it. If I'm helping my wife shop and someone turns down another aisle when they see me, I'm just going to leave that in Your hands. I don't know how to handle this; it's now Your responsibility."

This time I truly released my cares to the Lord. Instead of matters improving, they got worse. Ultimately the most hideous untruths were spread. I don't think anyone could possibly have thought up any worse gossip than what we endured.

The Gossip Backfires

At the factory where many of the stories were being spread, a strange turn of events occurred about a week later. The workers began to tire of hearing the endless stream of gossip. Soon they were saying, "Ah, leave me alone; I don't want to hear about all that junk going on at your church. Man, just leave me alone. I don't care about it."

But the gossips kept on talking. Those who listened began to notice how these few people were obsessed with criticism and filled with hatred. They also noticed that the Spirit-filled people they knew personally were not seething with anger. Instead, they were quite relaxed and loving by comparison. Observing this difference, the men at the factory began to think that the gossips were really the ones who were off base.

So the more the gossips kept at it, and the more their wives poured their venom over the telephone, the worse their reputations became. Their respectability gradually decreased while ours increased. In fact, my reputation continued to improve so much that I became somewhat of a hero in town. I did not deserve to be a hero, nor did I deserve to be looked up to, but the Lord allowed it. Even today the people of that town who know me hold me in very high regard. The Lord handled the problem far better than I could.

Letting Jesus Handle the Heat

The Lord's ways are often not our ways. But if we will only listen to Him and trust Him, He will work everything out for our good. As the verse goes on to say, "He shall bring it to pass" (Psalm 37:5). Isn't that beautiful?

Oh, the fire raged and the flames roared, trying in many ways to consume us. But we were at peace, just enjoying the warm glow. The gossips were the ones on tranquilizers, not us. While they were sickly and nervous, we were keeping cool in the midst of the flames.

I shared this priceless lesson with many others, and they took it to heart. We began to apply this principle in every little phase of life. Dumping all difficulties in the lap of Jesus and turning away from them became an easy, habitual way to respond to pressure. Life became almost too carefree. But that is the way life is when Jesus is in control. It *is* easy.

Most importantly, the furnace began to burn away the dross in our lives. We were overcoming our problems instead of having them overcome us. Much of the daily frustration of living disappeared as we learned to roll everything off onto the massive shoulders of Jesus. He took care of the heat, our problems, and our flesh.

CHAPTER SEVEN

Forgive Who For What?

The next year for our church was a wonderful one. Those who stood against us increased their pressure, but somehow this did not bother our group of Spirit-filled believers. The cooling protection of the Lord encircled us.

After that year of grace, though, we began to feel the heat again. The attacks were getting under our skin, and we started to swelter.

One day I went to my office (my usual place of prayer) to ask the Lord what was wrong. I really did not understand. "Lord," I prayed, "we are handing You our problems. But now they are a burden to us again. What has gone wrong?"

The familiar voice of the Father spoke within me and answered, "My son, you have not forgiven them completely." I was shocked. I said, "God, I forgive. Of course, I forgive them."

"Yes, you forgive them, but the reason you are feeling this heaviness is because your forgiveness is not complete."

"Then you will have to teach me how to forgive completely, Lord. I am willing to do it." Over the next few weeks God taught me what He meant by forgiveness. This valuable lesson was to forever protect me from all attacks of man.

I Will Forgive

The Lord said, "I want you to come before Me as a king coming before the King of kings, and officially pronounce them forgiven. I want it to be a definite act of your will. I do not want you just to say 'I forgive them' if I happen to ask you."

So that was what He meant. I went into the church sanctuary, turned on the lights, and stood before the altar. I cried, "Oh, God, as of this night (I named the date), I officially forgive them every single sin they have ever committed against me. I officially forgive them as a king before You, the King of kings, in Jesus' name. Amen."

"Forgive who?" the Lord asked.

"Well, Mr. so-and-so," I answered.

"Forgive him of what?" the Lord asked specifically.

"Oh, this and that." I began to name the hurts.

"Anything else?"

"Yes, there is this and this."

"Anything else?"

"Well, I can't think of anything else."

"Who else are you forgiving?" The Lord continued to probe.

"Well, there is his wife."

All at once it dawned on me. I walked over to the altar rail just as if each one of them were kneeling there. In my mind's eye, I went to each of them and laid my hands on their heads. I named the person and I named the sins one by one to God. I went down the row person by person and sin by sin until I officially had forgiven each offender and each offense before God. The more itemized the sins, the greater the release I experienced.

When I had finished, the pressure that was in my heart had lifted. A beautiful cleansing had occurred. I felt almost perfect but not quite. In a few days I realized my peace had not completely returned, so I went to my office for prayer.

Canceling I.O.U.'s

Again the Lord showed me my heart. I was overwhelmed to find that the problem was still in the area of forgiveness. Although I had officially forgiven my offenders before Him, my heart still cried, "You must pay." I realized that in the recesses of my heart I was holding a stack of I.O.U.'s against these people. I would not free my offenders from their debts until they knew how much they had hurt me.

God said, "Son, if you want peace, you must let them go. You must tear up the I.O.U.'s." As God gave this directive, I saw two things. First, I had iron bars in my chest with these people locked inside. I could forgive them, but I wasn't going to let them go because they owed me.

Second, I saw a great, huge bowl of flames, which I believe was the Holy Spirit. I needed to tear up these I.O.U.'s, which would immediately cancel the debt. Going one step further, I needed to throw them into the flames, letting the Holy Spirit burn them to ashes. So that I wouldn't try to recover even the charred remains, I was to let the wind of the Spirit scatter the ashes. That's a full, complete releasing. That's what the Lord was asking me to do.

Again I went into the sanctuary that evening and turned on the light. I stood before the altar. I said, "Lord, as a king before You, the King of kings, I officially release those gossips and I tear up all their I.O.U.'s. They don't owe me anything."

Down inside there were the words, "Tear up whose I.O.U.'s?" I realized the Lord wanted me to again go person by person and sin by sin. To tear up the whole pack of I.O.U.'s at once was official and would have counted for something, but it wouldn't have the same releasing power of canceling the specific debts of each individual. Had I suffered future hurts, somehow I'm sure I would have found in my pocket an extra I.O.U. that had not been torn up.

The Referee

I spent a lot of time going person by person and sin by sin, tearing up the I.O.U.'s. With each offender released and with each debt cancelled, I felt a heaviness breaking up inside of me. When I had finished, I felt so greatly relieved that the burden seemed gone. I felt almost perfect peace—but not quite.

A few days later I realized I still did not have the complete peace I had once known. Checking the peace of my heart was one way to know whether or not I was walking uprightly before the Lord. Colossians 3:15 says, "Let the peace of God rule in your hearts."

The Greek word for rule, *brabeuo,* is one which implies to watch over—to be a judge or a referee. If we have committed a foul, if our heart is not responding to the Lord, if we are not walking uprightly before Him, then we will lose our peace.

My lack of perfect peace indicated another problem, but this time I was really baffled. Surely now my forgiveness was perfected. Perhaps there was some other area of my life that was not right. As I prayed in my office, God said once again, "Bob, you have not forgiven them completely."

I was speechless. I had no idea what God meant. I know people who have lost their peace because they have not forgiven completely. These tormented souls are awake at night, not because of what others have done to them, but because of the animosity they're harboring in their hearts. We often think we've forgiven when we don't even really understand God's meaning of the word.

Forgive and Forget

I still did not understand. I said, "God, how can there be more? You will have to show me."

"My son, you must *forget* everything they have done."

"But, God, that is impossible! I can't. It's a historical fact that these things have happened. They are stored in my gray matter."

"My memory is better than yours. Yet, I forget *your* sins."

Then God said something I'll never forget. "Bob, your *will* is greater than your memory. You *will* forget the hurts, if you *will* to forget them."

The passage shot through my mind, "Casting down imaginations, and every high thing that exalteth itself against the knowledge of God, and bringing into captivity every thought to the obedience of Christ" (2 Corinthians 10:5). I understood then that I had to renounce those memories just as strongly as I would renounce any demon.

Once again I found myself standing before the altar. One by one I renounced the memories and asked forgiveness for having hung onto them for so long. After awhile I felt more freedom than I had in a long time.

I Won't Remember

That night as I was renouncing the hurtful memories, I had a nagging thought. "Lord, what if the memories creep back in?" I asked. Negative thoughts have a way of quietly surfacing in our minds, playing back hurtful experiences, and churning our emotions until they drag us down.

The Lord spoke to me and said, "Ask for an alarm system at the door of your mind." So, I prayed and said, "Holy Spirit, watch over the door of my mind. If one of those memories begins to come back, I want to catch it, renounce it, and drive it from me."

Over the next few months some thoughts had to be driven away repeatedly, but gradually they grew weaker and weaker until they disappeared. If I wanted to remember specific hurts, I would have to deliberately try to recall those incidents. But I refused to do it because it would have poisoned me and hurt my Lord and those people.

You see, it's not that God *can't* remember our sins. It's that He *won't* remember our sins. He has made a decision to forget them. He has deliberately blocked them out. He doesn't want to remember our sins any more.

There may be some very hurtful memories that you have to refuse to recall. Your mind may require months of driving those thoughts away every day before they gradually disappear, but believe me, it's worth the effort! Moreover, God demands forgiveness of his children if they are to be like Him.

How Many Times?

Peter approached Christ and asked, "Lord, how often shall my brother sin against me, and I forgive him? Up to seven times?" (Matthew 18:21, NKJV). Peter understood that forgiveness was involved, but was unsure of the extent of his actions. Jesus responded with a very surprising answer. "I do not say to you, up to seven times, but up to seventy times seven" (Matthew 18:22, NKJV).

Let's look at the corresponding account in Luke. "And if he [your brother] sins against you seven times in a day, and seven times in a day returns to you, saying, 'I repent,' you shall forgive him" (Luke 17:4, NKJV). Jesus said that this kind of forgiving should be done *daily.*

I find it hard to believe that someone could sin against me 490 times in a single day. A person would have to work at it to sin against me a hundred times a day. I can't imagine 490 times! Jesus said that we must continue to forgive no matter how often we are offended.

You Owe Me!

Jesus stressed the importance of releasing our offenders from their debts and the sobering consequences of unforgiveness when He told the parable of the unjust servant. That servant owed his master 10,000 talents (approximately 20 million dollars in today's money). Because he didn't have the means to repay, the king commanded that he and all of his family should be sold so that the payment could be made. The servant fell down before his king and said, "Master, have patience with me, and I will pay you all" (Matthew 18:23-26).

The master was moved with compassion, released the servant, and forgave him the debt. He didn't just say, "Okay, you can work it off." He forgave him the debt. But that servant went out and found one of his fellow servants who owed him a hundred denarii (the equivalent of a day's wage). He grabbed him by the throat, demanding, "Pay me what you owe" (Matthew 18:27,28).

Why would anyone do that? Most of us do not fully trust that our heavenly Father can forgive us the way He does, so we demand payment from one another.

Scripture says his fellow servant fell down at the man's feet saying, "Have patience with me and I will pay you all." But the other man would not listen, and had him thrown into prison until he paid the debt.

When his fellow servants saw what had happened, they were grieved. They told their master what had been done, and the master called the unjust servant and said to him, "You wicked servant! I forgave you all that debt because you begged me. Should you not also have had compassion on your fellow servant, just as I had pity on you?" His master was angry and delivered him to the tormentors until he paid all that was due to him.

Jesus said, "So My heavenly Father also will do to you if each of you, from his heart, does not forgive his brother his trespasses" (See Matthew 18:29-35).

Jesus, addressing believers, warned that His heavenly Father will turn even His children over to tormentors if they do not forgive their brothers every offense. That is a powerful statement. Not heeding God's command to forgive will destroy your soul.

Stabbing Ourselves with Unforgiveness

God turns people over to tormentors until they learn to forgive everybody of everything. Many

Christians are still under torment because they have forgiven partially but not completely. To the extent that an offended person has not forgiven, to that extent he is under torment. The peace of God will continue to elude his grasp until forgiveness is complete.

Some people even keep little mental file cards on all the sins a certain person has done to them. They have instant recall of sins from even years before. Though they have been Christians for a long time, they have not learned to forgive God's way. They pray the Lord's prayer, "Forgive us our trespasses as we forgive those who trespass against us," and they are still in knots, because they don't forgive completely.

When a person who has been repeatedly hurt by the same offender is wronged again, he seizes the sharp knife of unforgotten wounds and stabs himself again. The anguish of past hurts is added to the pain of new hurts, making it seem many times worse than it really is. Blame is placed squarely on the other person. No wonder relationships break down so easily.

Before I was saved, I used to write down the nasty things that my wife said on little slips of paper and hide them behind the socks in the upper drawer. That's not forgetting! No wonder my marriage was a mess in those days. Now I was learning to forgive far more than I had ever forgiven before. I forgave my wife and my children, my mother, my father, my brother, and everyone else who had ever hurt me. What a healing!

My friend, if you do not have peace in your heart, see if a residue of unforgiveness remains. What if you have forgiven ninety percent of the way, but have left that ten percent residue? Is it enough? The next hurt will leave another ten percent and the next another. Finally it will be impossible to forgive and you will be open to torment.

Here Comes One Now

My inner cleansing seemed almost, but not quite, perfect. A few days later, the nagging thought came that all was not well. I was amazed. I said, "God, I have forgiven them. Surely that is taken care of. I have done it officially. I have torn up the I.O.U.'s. I have renounced the memories. What is wrong? I don't understand. Is there some other area of my life You are trying to work on?"

Then came the words, "You have not forgiven them completely."

"No! That is impossible. Surely my forgiveness is complete." I was totally mystified.

Gently the Lord asked, "How do you feel when you see one of them walk into the church on Sunday?"

I had to admit I would feel, "Oh, no. Here comes one of them now." I had taken care of the specific sins, but I was nurturing some very negative generalized feelings about those people.

Once again I marched in before the altar. I had to renounce those feelings person by person. I especially had to ask forgiveness for having allowed those negative feelings to build up. I had to ask forgiveness for letting them poison my system. I'm glad that my heavenly Father does not harbor negative feelings toward me, but in His forgiveness He has kept his heart positive and open to me.

Negative feelings can rob us of such joy. The other person can often sense our heart and detects the underlying ill will. Those negative feelings keep the warfare going, fuel the animosity, and maintain the distance between us.

When I was finished, I felt clean and wonderful. I even danced around the chancel. But again, my heart was still not quite perfect, although I didn't realize it at the time.

After some days I felt that all was not well, and I sought the Lord for that perfect peace once again. I wondered what other areas of sin the Lord could be dealing with. Those same words reverberated in my spirit, "You have not forgiven them completely."

You could have knocked me over with a feather. How could this be? Surely the lesson was over. Then the Lord showed me one last thing to make my forgiveness complete. I had no idea what He meant, but I knew enough to listen.

Give Me Eyes of Compassion

"Son, do you remember the woman in Scripture who was possessed with seven demons?" the Lord asked me.

"Yes, Lord,"

"Can you imagine what kind of a life she must have lived being possessed with seven demons?"

"Lord, it must have been a horrible life, hurting herself, her family, and others."

"Why didn't she go to the synagogue to get help?"

I thought about it and asked, "Why, Lord?"

"Many of them may have wanted to help her, but had she walked through the door of the synagogue, they would have looked at her as a woman possessed with seven demons. She couldn't bear to face their judgmental stares, so she never went.

"Why did she approach Me? Why did all those harlots and publicans crowd around Me? Why did they want to be with Me? Why did they want Me to come to their house to eat?"

I was amazed at the question. Jesus is far more holy and righteous than the people of the synagogue, and yet these sinners wanted to be near Him.

"When I looked at her, I didn't see her as a woman possessed with seven demons. I saw her as the beautiful Mary Magdalene she was meant to be. That's the look she saw in My face, and that's why she came.

"My son, that's the way I want you to look at all of those who have hurt you. I want you to see them as they are when they are cleansed in Me."

I began to weep. How far I had been from forgiving as I was supposed to forgive. How far I had been from having a heart of compassion like the Lord. No wonder I had been in torment.

"Oh, God, help me to see them the way You do. Give me those eyes of compassion, give me Your eyes." Daily I and many others in our group prayed this prayer. Gradually it happened. More and more we were able to see those who had hurt us through God's eyes.

The spirit-filled people and I began to change so much that when those who fought us came to church on Sunday morning we were happy to see them. We wanted to run up and give them a holy hug. Of course, we never did that because the people wouldn't understand. Our hearts ached for them.

A Giant Step Forward

Sometime later the Lord taught me still another point on forgiving people. Our forgiveness must be a justifying forgiveness if it is to be like His. When God forgives, He treats us like we had never sinned against Him in the first place. In God's eyes a repentant person has never hurt Him.

God doesn't do that because He found some reason in us that justifies our having sinned. He simply reckons us as being justified. The word is *dikaioo* in the Greek. To have an *oo* ending on a Greek word means that is the way God perceives us. He is simply declaring us righteous—not that we actually were. Since that is the way God sees us, that is the way He treats us—as though we had never sinned in the first place.

That's how God wants us to forgive our offenders—as if they had never hurt us in the first place. The cross of Christ is our motivation for forgiving. Because Jesus has taken the punishment for their sins—including their sins against us— we must look at their innocence and treat them as if they had never wronged us in any way.

Now, at last, we enjoyed the peace of God in our lives. We were able to quickly forgive not just the big hurts, but all the little irritations that people gave us. God drew us another giant step closer to being overcomers.

What a tremendous lesson! The gold must be tried in the fire to come out pure before God. The dross must rise to the surface and burn away. There is a reason you go through the flames of pressure.

You must realize that you are not in the pit; you are not cut off from God; you are merely in His furnace.

Of course, it may be the same old problems that used to destroy you in the pit, but now they are only meant to purge the dross, to change you, and to mold you. As self is dealt a death blow, you will experience newness of life in Christ and His overcoming power. Praise God for the furnace. Respond to it His way, and you will keep cool in the hottest flames.

CHAPTER EIGHT

Increase Our Love, Lord

Within a few months hardly an offense could penetrate our wall of forgiveness. Our little group had become adept at forgiving and had learned to forget immediately. Wrongs and sins seemed to bounce off us almost immediately. But gradually we found how pressures from our congregation melted away our peace.

I was driven once more to that place of soul-searching that had become my classroom. This time, instead of taking weeks, the lesson was over in ten minutes—and those ten minutes dramatically transformed my life.

Deep inside me there were words. They were alive and they shook me to the core. As I was praying about my problems, God said, "Bob, the reason you are so upset is because you do not love them enough."

There was a time when I could have acknowledged what the Lord meant by not loving enough. I had not loved at all. But that was another time, another world, another man. Now I said, "God, I do love them. I could not forgive them if I did not love them. You have been building love in me all these years."

"But the reason you are feeling the pressure is because you do not love them enough."

"Then teach me how to love," I cried. There was no answer. Only silence filled the room. I sat at my desk bewildered, not knowing what to do. My mind was churning over the words the Lord had just spoken.

In desperation I flipped my Bible open and began to read. My eyes fell upon John 17, the great high priestly prayer of Jesus. This beautiful prayer is so rich and powerful. One could make a sermon out of every verse, yet I hardly noticed the words because of the turmoil in my mind.

Then my eyes fell on verse 23. "That the world may know that You have sent Me, and have loved them as You have loved Me." The words leaped off the page and exploded somewhere inside me. I had experienced this type of revelation a number of times, but never like that—not even John 3:16 on the day I was saved.

Loved Like Jesus

Jesus prayed to the Father in heaven, not just for His disciples but for those who would believe on Him through their words. (See John 17:20.) Because I had believed on Him through their word, Jesus was praying for me. Yet He went on to say in verse 23 that the Father loves us as He loves Jesus.

"God, how can that be? How can You love me as You love Jesus? I do not understand. Oh, God, I have sinned against You every day of my life. I have been proud, selfish, and rebellious. How can You love me like that?"

"My son, that is what the cross was all about." The Father's powerful words filled my being.

Now I had known what the cross was about since the day I was saved. But one can know it and still learn more about it. I had not seen until now how the cross had opened the way to God's love for me. This truth was almost more than I could grasp.

Again I cried, "How can this be? I have failed You again and again. As a minister, as a father, as a husband, as a son. How could You love me as You love Jesus?"

"My son, that is what the cross was all about," the Lord repeated. "When you hand your failings to Me, I turn them around 180 degrees and make blessings out of them."

My mind was churning as God performed some kind of spiritual surgery inside me as those words took root. My heart still asked, "Why? I'm not like Jesus. How could You love me as You did Him?"

He spoke, "My love is given by grace and not by works. I simply love you with all My heart."

No More Jealousy

I melted and wept before the words of God. Finally, I was silent for a while, trying to take it all in. I sensed that God desired to reveal more about my own personal life. Then He opened my eyes to a most thrilling realization.

Deep inside me the Lord spoke sovereignly again and pointed out that if He loved me as He loved Jesus, then wouldn't He love me as He loved the apostle Paul and Moses? As He loves Pat Robertson and Billy Graham? As He loves Chuck Swindoll and James Dobson? He said, "You don't need to feel jealous of them anymore." (God knew me better than I knew myself.)

There was no reason for me to hang onto my jealousy—jealousy that I would not even admit to myself. How foolish to be jealous or envious when we already have all His love! We are not in competition for God's love. The great heart of God loves us just the way we are.

Reaching up with my hands as if to take this great load of jealousy off my shoulders, I threw it down and cried out to God to forgive me. I was ashamed. As the burden lifted, I knew I did not have to be afraid of people getting ahead of me or outshining me. I was fully loved. I did not have to earn love or fight for it. God loved me the same way and as much as He loved Jesus.

Oh, friend, do not allow jealousy to creep into your life. If you sing in the choir and someone sings a little better than you do, praise God for it. If you are a preacher and another preacher has a more powerful ministry than you, praise God for it. We are not in competition; we are all on the same team. We need each other, and there is certainly enough work for everybody.

No More Pride

As I waited quietly, the Lord also pointed out that I had looked down on others who seemed less spiritual. Those who did not pray, read their Bibles, and witness as they should were loved by God just as much as He loved Jesus—and me. I repented of that pride and cast it away as I had the jealousy. What folly to be proud. What uselessness. We are all completely loved. The body of Christ began to take on a new meaning for me.

As these thoughts were taking hold, God spoke one more time. He asked, "My son, if My love is given by grace and not by works, then don't I love those in the congregation who have been

fighting against you and against My work?'' (The
Lord had shown me that all except about three of
them had saving faith. The majority were His children, but they were gripped by fear.) God asked
me, "Don't I love them as I have loved you, as I
love Jesus?"

"Yes, Lord, You must."

"Then love them as I have loved you!"

What a joy to see the love of God in this way!
What a cleansing and healing effect it had.

More Love

As I shared this revelation with others in the
group, we began to pray for God to increase our
love.

As we thanked God for those who attacked and
persecuted us, we stopped looking at our problems as bad and unfair. Instead we saw the beautiful work God wanted to create in us as we
yielded to His way in our lives.

In the months ahead we sought the Lord to give
us more love. Love does, indeed, cover a multi-
tude of sins. (See 1 Peter 4:8.) Loving is not just
something that happens to us by osmosis—we
have to fervently ask the Lord for it. God must create it within us, for love is not a fruit of our own
efforts.

We must seek after, covet, and earnestly desire
love more than any of the gifts of the Spirit. Love

is "a more excellent way" as 1 Corinthians 12:31 says, so desire and hunger after love. Daily in prayer we asked for love with increasingly hungry hearts.

Most people who experience difficulty in giving love are people who have had trouble receiving love. As youngsters they may have been shortchanged. Their fathers and mothers may have never hugged them or expressed love in tangible ways. These children may have had enough love to get by and cope with life, but their hearts are aching.

Perhaps their parents pushed them to be achievers at an early age, and these children grew up thinking they had to earn love. They always felt inferior—like they couldn't quite make it.

Perhaps their parents beat them or called them names like "stupid," and they grew up believing it. Because they've never learned how to receive love, they've never learned how to give it. Their hearts are aching and torn, and they've never known happiness or peace. How can they experience the love of God? Let me tell you how one woman received the assurance of God's love for her.

Making Up the Difference

On one of my trips to the South American jungles I stopped in the city of Medellin, Columbia, where I was invited to speak at a seminary. Because the students didn't know about the baptism of the Holy Spirit, I decided to share my experience and the teachings of Scripture on this subject.

At the end of my message the director of the seminary leaped to his feet and exclaimed, "This is the thing we've been missing! This is the reason why we don't have power when we witness!" He called the whole student body and the staff to their knees to receive the baptism of the Spirit with the laying on of hands. That night there was a tremendous, powerful revival.

After the meeting, the director asked me to come to his house and pray with his wife. He said, "I love my wife, and our children love her, but for years she has had to take medication because of her deep depression."

The director's wife, who was five feet two inches tall and about as big around, met us at the front door. When I saw the blank expression on her face, I realized she had a serious problem.

Not knowing what to do or say, I quickly prayed, "Lord, give me Your words. Let me know what I need to say to her." Immediately God quickened to me Psalm 27:10 that says if your father and mother forsake you, the Lord will take you up. That means if a person has been turned away, rejected, or just shortchanged in love by their parents that the Lord would make up the difference.

I turned to this lady, explained that passage of Scripture, and said, "When you grew up, you did not receive enough love from your parents. Although they loved you, they didn't know how to express it. I'm going to pray over these next months, day by day, that you will hear the whisper of your heavenly Father telling you how much He loves you.

"You can't go back and be a little girl. You can't crawl up on your daddy's lap and say, 'Oh, Daddy, please give me the love I need. Oh, Mommy, please love me.' It's too late for that. But the Lord will make up the difference. I'm going to pray that the word He whispers in your heart will be a creative word that will heal your wounds and create in you the love that is missing."

So I prayed that simple prayer. The next day I heard that she woke up in the morning singing, bouncing all around, feeling happy and full of life. She hadn't been that way in over five years.

Not long ago I heard that she is still full of life and stronger than ever. You see, the Lord had whispered into her heart how much He loved her. His words were full of creative life. Day by day while she read the Bible, prayed, and even did the dishes, God revealed His love until her heart and mind were healed.

Many people who have been shortchanged on love don't know that God's love is there for the asking. Pray and ask the heavenly Father to make up to you any deficit of love that you may have experienced as a youngster. Listen for His whisper and let His words create the needed healing in your heart.

CHAPTER NINE

Where Does Love Come From?

Love often requires a conscious decision. Love is an act of our will. You do not just fall in love with someone. That is a false concept. You do not stumble over love—it does not sneak up behind you and trip you. You grow in love. And it starts with a decision to love.

I often counsel with women who say, "I can no longer love my husband." These women loved their husbands when they were first married, but somewhere along the way they stopped loving them because their husbands were so unlovable.

I ask them, "When did you decide not to love your husband?" These wives deny ever having made such a decision. When I point out that by an unconscious decision they had allowed their love to die, perhaps as a punishment for his extreme selfishness, many of these women break in tears of repentance.

My friend, love begins and ends with a decision. When you were still a single person, you made a conscious or unconscious decision to find someone with whom to fall in love. When you saw a man or woman whom you admired, you decided to get to know him or her better. Perhaps you wanted to see what they were really like. You may have thought they were good marriage material.

If you discovered that they were going steady, or engaged to someone else, you said, "Well, it has been nice knowing you," and then went on your way. You turned off any emotions that were beginning to rise in you. You deliberately, by an act of your will, set those feelings aside. The decision to love or not to love might come in small stages, but it is a deliberate act, and your will plays the active part.

You may need to make a deliberate decision before God to rekindle your love toward someone who has hurt you. You may need to make a decision to receive love from them. Do it! And watch how God changes your heart. The Lord loves to back up such decisions. You will discover a whole new array of feelings for that other person.

Deciding to Love

This truth was made clear to me when I attended a leaders' conference. The goal of this conference was to help people grow in Spirit-filled living and develop in leadership. In an effort "to be fair," however, the program committee had invited some speakers who were not only non-charismatic but anti-charismatic.

Many of us who had gone to the conference to be edified became highly upset. I could feel my anger rising rapidly. By the second day I found it hard to love those speakers who were so against the charismatic renewal. Avoiding Scripture, they presented their "logical" arguments and gave what they thought was an "honest" approach.

I admitted belatedly that my emotions were getting out of control and that my building resentment was more of a problem than the speakers. I finally went to a close friend and repented to God in his presence, asking for his prayers and his personal pronouncement of forgiveness as an ambassador of Christ. With my friend's help and absolution I was able to overcome the loveless feelings that had been growing.

But as I returned to the conference, another speaker began taking his "potshots" at the "tongues movement" as he called it. All the old feelings welled up again, and the battle resumed. Unable to bear it, I left the room and sought a place to be alone with God. There, in frustration, I sought Him.

"God, what is wrong? Why can't I control these feelings of anger?"

The answer came clearly, "You must reign over the situation. You must make a deliberate decision before Me to love them." Again I thought of myself as a king making a royal decision before the King of kings.

When I did, all the strength I needed to love them suddenly welled up within me. God used my decision to tear out the roots of bitterness. When I returned to the conference those speakers had not changed, but I had. I could have given each of those men a holy hug. What tremendous change the Lord wrought in me when I set my heart and made a decision to love.

Focus on the Father's Love

Once I learned this lesson, the doors of love seemed to swing wide open. I began to see love in a new way. My dear old friend Linn Haitz, who had prayed daily for years that God would increase his love, said, "Bob, we have always focused on the love of Jesus at the cross, but I wonder if we have really seen the love of the Father.

"Can you imagine Jesus in the garden praying, beseeching the Father with all His might, so burdened that His sweat came as great drops of blood? He was in utter agony of soul. He was praying harder than He had ever prayed in His life.

"If God had ever heard anyone's prayers, He heard Jesus'. If God ever loved anyone, He loved

Jesus. This was His Son in whom He was well pleased. Three times Jesus besought the Father, 'If it be possible, if there is any other way, let this cup pass from Me. Nevertheless, not My will but Thine be done.' ''

Linn continued, ''Bob, we can see Jesus' love there, willing to go through it all. But have you ever noticed the love of the Father who, although His heart must have been aching for His Son, let Jesus go all the way? No doubt twelve legions of angels had their hands on the hilts of their fiery swords, ready to help Jesus and to turn this world into ashes. I am sure the Father's heart groaned at Jesus' cries. Yet He loved *us* so much that He never wavered from His purpose. He never sent the angels to deliver His Son. What measureless love our Father has for us.''

Embraced by His Love

One passage that the Holy Spirit used to show me the Father's love is from the Psalms.

> As a father pitieth his children, so the Lord pitieth them that fear him. For he knoweth our frame. He remembereth that we are dust—Psalm 103:13,14.

The Hebrew word for pity is *racham,* meaning to hold tightly or caress. Sometimes racham is used for the word womb where the unborn baby is kept safe, nurtured, and protected.

To picture *racham,* imagine a little girl walking hand in hand with her father through crowds of people at the circus or carnival. She catches a glimpse of a clown carrying balloons, lets go of her father's hand, and darts through the crowd.

Her father calls and dashes after her, but she runs to find the clown. Then she is easily distracted by something else and zigzags in a different direction. Pretty soon she's lost. Eventually she realizes that she is alone, and the thought "Where's Daddy?" jolts her to her senses. Now she's not interested in anything about the carnival—she wants Daddy!

With tears streaming down her cheeks, she frantically looks for Daddy in the shuffling crowd. People are asking, "Can I help you, little girl?" but she doesn't pay any attention to them. At last out of the crowd Daddy appears. "Oh, there you are, sweetheart!" he exclaims. He gathers her up in his arms and hugs her tight. All her insides just sigh and say, "Oh, Daddy!" That's *racham*. That's the way the Father wants to hold us.

Because God knows our frame, He realizes we're but dust. He didn't make us out of granite so that we're never tossed about by the storms of life. He made us out of dust, which crumbles easily under pressure. He knows we get blown about with the storms. God is our rock, our strength, and our fortress. He wants to hold us tightly because He loves us so much.

No Strings Attached

The extent of Jesus' love is expressed in one of His discourses to His disciples. "As the Father hath loved me, so have I loved you" (John 15:9). Jesus also loves us as the Father loves Him—perfectly and in every way. Our opinions of ourselves make it seem impossible, but the Word of God says it.

One day the Lord put the crowning touch on this lesson we were learning about His love. The family that had started the trouble in our congregation and had, through the years, remained one of the chief antagonists, was having a very difficult time. The wife, battling cancer, had endured seventeen operations on her throat over a period of fourteen years. The scar tissue had closed her throat so that she could drink only liquids. Then she could no longer drink and had to be fed intravenously. She was slipping away little by little.

Her husband was in her hospital room one evening, earnestly beseeching the Lord to help her. Although he had opposed much of what God was doing, he was a Christian and loved the Lord. Suddenly Jesus came into the room and appeared to him. In this heavenly vision Jesus held his hand as the husband prayed and wept.

By morning his wife was sitting up and able to eat. Her strength returned and soon she was well enough to be discharged from the hospital. The man to this day has never changed his stand; in fact, he still doesn't believe in divine healing. But Jesus loves him anyway with all His heart.

Jesus' love is not based on our purity, nor on our right theology, nor on our faithfulness to Him, nor on our great spiritual strength, nor on how little we have hurt Him. He simply loves us with all His heart; it is by grace. Oh, for a heart of love like that!

Love Me or Like Me?

At this time I began a study of love in the Scriptures. I noticed that the Bible repeatedly uses two terms for our one term *love*: *agape* and *philia*.

Most Bible teachers whom I have heard preach on love have called the *philia* love a brotherly love or family love or companionship love. I found that this is not completely accurate. *Philadelphia* is the Greek word that means "brotherly love." But *philia* by itself is simply a love where you set your heart upon something or someone.

A man can have *philia* love for money if he sets his heart upon it. This is the word used in 1 Timothy 6:10, "The love of money is the root of all evil." An engaged couple often have this kind of love for each other; all they can think of is one another.

I began to wonder if God had that kind of love for me. I knew He had *agape* love for me—that sacrificial love, the giving love that asks nothing in return. But could He ever have *philia* love for a character like me? Could He ever like me? Surely I did not deserve to have Him set His heart upon me. Surely I am not worthy of that.

As I prayed, the thought came to me, "Look it up." I discovered that Jesus said, "The Father Himself loves *[phileo]* you" (John 16:27, NKJV). Hallelujah! He likes me!

Suddenly, the Holy Spirit brought to mind a flood of passages that describe us as "the apple of God's eye" and the "jewels in His crown." He reminded me of a most touching passage:

> Can a woman forget her nursing child and not have compassion on the son of her womb? Surely they may forget, yet I will not forget you. See, I have inscribed you on the palms of My hands; your walls are continually before Me—Isaiah 49:15,16, NKJV.

We are branded into the hand of God. He involves us in everything His hand finds to do. The walls of our lives are continually before the Lord.

He sees all we're struggling with, all we're going through, and all we're trying to build. The only thing He doesn't see is our sins. God has cast away our transgressions and will remember them no more.

The Lord also quickened these passages to me:

> "For I know the thoughts that I think toward you, says the Lord, thoughts of peace and not of evil, to give you a future and a hope"—Jeremiah 29:11, NKJV.

> The Lord has appeared of old to me, saying: "Yes, I have loved you with an everlasting love; therefore with loving-kindness I have drawn you"—Jeremiah 31:3, NKJV.

Oh, my heart burst to hear the Lord whispering these words in my heart! I was loved; I was delighted in; I was liked. His heart had wrapped itself around me.

Empowered by Love

What a powerful love philia is! Philia is the strength that makes agape do its work. Isn't it easy to sacrifice for someone if we delight in them?

When we like people, it is hard to think negatively of what they say and do. Philia love makes friendships so strong.

I discovered that philia love, like agape, is there for the asking. God will increase it in us if we want Him to.

At one period in my married life, Letitia and I were drifting apart. We began to quarrel and see things differently. I asked the Lord what was wrong and what could be done. The Lord answered, "Ask for *philia* love."

I said "All right, Lord."

At the time I was unaware of its power, but every day I began to pray, "Lord, give me philia love for my wife. Let me like her. Let me delight in her." God gave it to me. Within a few weeks philia love became so strong in me that my wife could see it in my eyes. She began to melt. Soon she started to love me back. Our marriage was healed.

Philia love is so strong and so healing that it makes marriages work and congregations flow smoothly. We must never think lightly of philia love. Keep this type of love in your prayers because it is important and worth the sacrifice.

God's Greatest Desire

As I thought about all of this, I could not help asking, "What is God getting out of it all?" When it is all over, when that great day has come and Jesus takes us to our heavenly home, what is God going to get for His trouble, His efforts, His patience? All He will get is *us.* He is not desirous of the gold or the silver—just us. He has set His heart upon us. His whole purpose, direction, and goal is in us. That is how great His love is!

No wonder Jesus wanted to get close to sinners. They were the objects of His desire. He talked to them, ate with them, and He still does. He stands at the door and knocks, and if anyone opens his heart to Him, He says, "I will come in to him and will sup with him" (Revelation 3:20). No wonder He looked over the city of Jerusalem that was soon to reject Him and wept for it.

The only thing that prevents you from loving more is your slowness to appreciate how much you are loved by Him. If you could only turn your eyes from your own unworthiness and look to His love, how much more rapid would be your growth, how much greater your capacity for love!

CHAPTER TEN

Changing the Way We Think

I once read an article in *Reader's Digest* about a certain hill in Vietnam. This hill was held by a company of marines against hordes of Viet Cong and North Vietnamese. Even in hand-to-hand combat these courageous marines tenaciously held their ground. When relief finally came, the twelve surviving marines were taken back to their base. These brave men were the most decorated outfit in the Vietnam War.

Why had these soldiers fought so desperately to maintain their stand? Because that hill overlooked an important valley through which the enemy sent supplies to its troops. The Viet Cong lost hundreds of lives attempting to take the hill. If the marine stronghold was left unchallenged, their supply route would be virtually cut off.

Our minds are like the high hill that holds the pass against the enemy. All opposing forces meet in the mind. Thoughts from our inner man surface in the mind. Conversations with people,

stories from the newspaper, and images from a bill-
board converge in the mind. The devil's temptations as well as God's thoughts enter through this
same doorway. Whoever *holds* that high ground
of the mind and keeps it from the enemy will
experience the victory of a transformed life.

The apostle Paul admonished the Roman
church:

> Be not conformed to this world: but be
> ye transformed by the *renewing of your
> mind,* that ye may prove what is that
> good, and acceptable, and perfect, will
> of God—Romans 12:2, italics added.

Handling the Heat

To be an overcomer we must have the mind of
Christ. How else can we be transformed into His
image? Imperfect thinking, negative outlooks, and
un-Christlike mental processes can make the furnace of testing seem hotter than it really is.

Many of the truths we learn from the Lord seem
easy to understand, yet are hard to put into practice in our daily lives. The difficulty comes not
in the magnitude of the trouble but in our mental
approach to handling the trouble. Because our
philosophies and outlook are different from God's
way of thinking, we are often overwhelmed in the

midst of the furnace. People attack us, but our minds magnify their actions.

The mind has tremendous power to make one mentally disturbed or physically ill. There are more than fifty common physical diseases partially or entirely attributed to bad thinking—including heart attacks, high blood pressure, ulcers, nervous stomachs, even arthritis, and some forms of cancer.

There is a well-known story of a philosopher who sat at the gate of a city. When a traveler approached the city and asked him what manner of place it was, the philosopher inquired, "What kind of city did you come from?" The newcomer might say, "Why, it was a terrible place. The people were mean. It was hard to get along with my neighbors." The wise man would answer, "That is exactly how it is here."

Another traveler might respond, "Why, the city I come from is wonderful; I hated to leave it. I truly enjoyed living there." The philosopher then replied, "That is exactly the kind of city this is." Far from lying or playing games, this philosopher knew one great truth—life is very much as we perceive it.

Proverbs 23:7 says, "For as he thinks in his heart, so is he" (NKJV). As a man sees himself in his inner being, that is what he will become. Therefore, we need the mind of Christ in one very important area—how we see ourselves. If we would be like Christ, we must see ourselves with the mind of Christ.

The Principle that Works

The secular world utilizes this principle. I remember watching Mark Spitz win gold medal after gold medal in the swimming events at the Munich Olympics. A sportscaster interviewed this superb athlete about his preparation for the competition. What helped him to become a winner? In practice Mark Spitz pictured himself ahead of all the other swimmers, outdistancing the competition. Mark Spitz could see himself winning.

When I heard his competitors being interviewed, they would say, "I know I can't beat Mark Spitz, but if I could just win a silver or a bronze medal . . ." Sure enough, they got only a silver or bronze medal. Their minds had set their own performance level.

When a football coach is in the dressing room before a game, he doesn't say, "Now team, I know our opponents are mighty tough and have a good record. I know we can't possibly win, but get in there and try to score at least one touchdown." The coach knows that if he said something like that, his team would probably get only one touchdown.

Instead the coach says, "I don't care how highly rated our opponents are. You're just as good as they are. You're just as strong as they are. Now get out there and show them. Hit 'em hard!'' Their problem is that the coach of the other team is saying the same thing. Coaches know that as a player thinks of himself in his heart, so he plays.

This principle is not limited to athletics. A little boy might say to his dad, "I cannot do math; I do not understand arithmetic. I will never be able to work these problems." As long as he thinks that way, math will be an insurmountable task. An older person who says, "I cannot remember names," will never improve his power of recall as long as he thinks this way.

Some Christians live far below their potential level of spirituality and closeness to God because of how they perceive themselves. All of us can picture ourselves reacting to a given set of circumstances in a particular way. For many of us our self-image is a very pitiful and defeat-filled picture.

Christians often identify themselves with sin, weakness, and failure. They say, "Oh, I could never witness. I cannot pray out loud. Those things are for someone else. I am just a wretch. I let God down so much. I am such a failure."

As long as they talk that way, they *will* have many sins, they *will* be poor, miserable wretches, and in many cases they *will* become failures. "As he thinketh in his heart, so is he" (Proverbs 23:7). These Christians find themselves far below the level at which God desires them to live. They have robbed themselves of blessings.

Defeated from the Start

What if David had allowed himself to think along those lines? Picture the time he brought food to his brothers in the army when they were battling the Philistines. The story might have had an entirely different ending. He might have never even become king if the situation had gone something like this.

Suppose David had approached his eldest brother and asked, "How's the battle going?" His brother said, "Why, it's terrible! Haven't you heard? Each day a giant from the opposing army challenges us to send someone out to fight with him. He also blasphemes our God. Look! There he is."

What if David had begun to let his mind think negatively? Suppose David had responded, "You're right. He is big! Look at the size of that spear!" If David had allowed such thoughts to creep in, he never would have gone down into that valley. He would have been as afraid as the others.

But David had learned not to allow that kind of thinking. He had walked with God and had come to see himself with God's eyes.

This is what the apostle Paul meant when he said, "Be ye transformed by the renewing of your mind" (Romans 12:2). You must start thinking as Jesus thinks.

David said, "Well, why doesn't someone go down and beat Goliath? God is with us." So David showed them and overcame the giant.

If we meditate on discouraging thoughts and focus on our unworthiness and shortcomings, we will be laid low. Instead of being overcomers, we will sink into depression and despair. Lacking courage, we will be unable to serve the Lord effectively. Our mental outlook has a tremendous influence on how we face the giants in our lives.

Too often Christians act like they are members of the Adams family. The first Adam was created righteous and holy. His disobedience brought a curse into the world, plus defeat, sickness, weakness, and death. Many Christians identify with the failing family of Adam and act accordingly. Some believers see themselves no different than anyone else except that someday, by and by, they and a few others will go to heaven while the rest go to hell.

These believers do not realize they have been adopted out of the Adams family into the Jesus family. Becoming a Christian involves living in a whole new existence—a whole new dimension. Believers sit with Christ in the heavenlies. (See Ephesians 2:6.) They are a royal priesthood. (See 1 Peter 2:9.) They are kings.

What God Wants for You

How does the Lord Himself look at you? In the middle of teaching a Bible class I saw a passage that gave me a completely new outlook on what God wants for His children.

> But I determined this within myself, that I would not come to you again in sorrow. For if I make you sorrowful, then who is he who makes me glad but the one who is made sorrowful by me?
> And I wrote this very thing to you, lest, when I came, I should have sorrow over those from whom I ought to have joy, having confidence in you all that my joy is the joy of you all—2 Corinthians 2:1-3, NKJV.

As I studied that passage it looked very complicated at first. I only got a few surface things out of it. But as I read it to the class, suddenly a veil seemed to lift from my eyes. I could hear the Father whispering to me, and I understood what He was saying.

The apostle Paul had written a very stern letter to the Corinthian Christians because they were sinning in many ways and refusing to repent. After having repented, they were sorry for their sins.

Paul wrote to them saying he would rather come to them now and make them glad than to weigh them down with heaviness. Paul preferred to have them rejoice than be cast down.

The Corinthian church had many problems, sins, and weaknesses that were not yet straightened out. So what is God saying through the apostle Paul?

God wants His children to be at peace. That's the priority in the father heart of God. He also wants them cleansed and healed, but once they have repented it's more important that they're rejoicing than struggling for perfection. God knows that when you're at peace and happy in the Lord, you will seek His help in the weak and sinful areas of your life.

I had never looked at God from that perspective. I thought that He always watched me with a critical eye and wanted to beat me into shape. Deep inside, I knew that God let hundreds of things go by without saying a word to me. When He finally pointed out one area, I would see what I had been doing wrong and repent of my sin. God never nagged me or worked on too many areas at once. I never could have endured it. God wants us to have peace.

If this is God's attitude toward us, how are we to see our children, our loved ones, and ourselves?

Freed from Negative Thinking

We are not to focus on our weaknesses, our defeats, and our sicknesses. We are new creatures. Let's stop holding Jesus at arm's length. Let's stop thinking about *our* weaknesses and start thinking about *His* strength. Jesus brought victory instead of defeat, blessing instead of cursing, joy instead of misery, and life instead of death.

If we, as Christians, would stand in front of a mirror just two minutes a day and confess to ourselves what God Himself is confessing about us in the Scriptures—that we are royal, holy, God's own children; that we are bone of Jesus' bone and flesh of His flesh; that we have authority over all the power of the enemy—what a new vision we would have of ourselves! Our thinking and our lives would be transformed. What strength we would have to face our trials. How quickly faith would grow. How much easier it would be to overcome.

If the old negative thoughts begin to creep back, rebuke them and cast them away in Jesus' name.

> Casting down imaginations, and every high thing that exalteth itself against the knowledge of God, and bringing into captivity every thought to the obedience of Christ—2 Corinthians 10:5.

Every time you do it, those strongholds will get progressively weaker.

Ask for an alarm system at the door of your mind to consciously catch the negative thoughts before they begin to overwhelm you. Yield your mind to the Holy Spirit. Ask Him to set a watch at the doorway so that at the very first negative or self-condemning thoughts you can catch them and rebuke them in the name of Jesus.

Soon these thoughts will have lost their power, and you will be free. You will have won the greatest of victories! You can go on to live a much finer, more beautiful life than ever before. This is not just the power of positive thinking. It is Jesus' power to set you free, to destroy negative thinking, and to create the mind of Christ in you.

CHAPTER ELEVEN

Combating a Critical Spirit

Since I was a little boy, I have always followed the elections. A number of years ago, I began to notice a significant change in our political campaigns. Each election year the candidates were using less and less energy telling the people what they stood for and what they wanted to do. More of their efforts were being spent finding fault with their opponents. Many speeches emphasized only what mistakes the other party had made. The candidates began to hire teams of men to look through the past records of their opponents in hope of finding some garbage with which to smear them.

A great demonic spirit of criticism has been loosed upon this nation. Fault-finding cynicism is prevalent almost everywhere, and its effects are devastating.

You can see the effects of criticism on the American home. In 1870 only one out of thirty marriages ended in divorce. By the turn of the century, it was one out of twelve. By 1930 it was one out of six. By 1960, one out of three. In many areas of the country most marriages now end in divorce. The spirit of criticism is one of the most destructive forces involved in the rapid and dramatic breakdown of the home—and as the home goes, so goes the society.

Criticism runs in a vicious, downward spiral that cuts deeper and wider with each person it touches. Suppose a man on his way to work in the morning pulls up to a stop sign but sticks out into the intersection a little too far. The driver of a milk truck coming down the other street is forced to swing a little wider to make his turn. He shakes his fist at the man blocking the intersection.

"Well, why did he do that?" says the man in the car. "I bet he does the same thing himself all the time. Who does he think he is?"

He shoves the car into gear and drives the next two blocks to work. In the parking lot he slams his car door and storms into the building still slamming doors.

Mary, the receptionist, smiles and greets him with a cheery "Good morning." With a grumble he reluctantly responds, "Yeah, good morning," and marches into his office, still angry.

Helen, a secretary, strolls by and asks Mary, "Hi, how are you?" When she gets no reply, Helen turns on her heel and under her breath says, "Well, I wonder what's wrong with her today!"

All through the day there are little, sharp barbs on the words that go flicking back and forth between co-workers. This becomes a drain on everyone at the office, and it turns out to be "one of *those* days." The sharp critical outlook has spread from one to another and has dragged many down.

At the end of the day, the man leaves the office irritable, exhausted, and worn out. He has long since forgotten what started it all. As he enters his home, he closes the front door with a bang. The wife in the kitchen looks up and sighs, "Oh, no, not another one of *those* days." Sure enough, it turns out to be another one of those evenings, as well. And so criticism spreads like a cancer.

Criticism Always Backfires

Unconsciously spreading into the minds of people across our nation is this spirit of backbiting—looking for faults in one another, digging out weaknesses, and pointing them out. The growing tendency can become an unbreakable habit. Fault finding is a sin that the Christian must totally overcome.

Becoming critical seems to momentarily relieve the pressure that one's own weaknesses have created. We seek to blame others for a flat tire, a broken mixer blade, and no milk in the refrigerator at breakfast. But to downgrade someone else never relieves the pressure, nor solves the problem, nor upgrades us.

We also have within us a self-defense mechanism to always prove we are right. But when we try to justify ourselves, we usually say to the other person that he is wrong. In order to prove that he is right, he more forcefully defends his side of the argument. This puts us on the defensive even more. And so the conflict only escalates. Criticism does not work, even in the guise of self-defense.

There is a spiritual principle that is an absolute with God. In fact, it is as reliable as the law of gravity. Jesus Himself said:

> "For with what judgment you judge,
> you will be judged; and with the same
> measure you use, it will be measured
> back to you"—Matthew 7:2, NKJV.

Whatever we dish out, we are going to get back. If we dish out criticism, it will return to us. If we are critical with our children now, they may not be able to fight back, but wait until they're sixteen. God's principles work.

Our tendency to correct our loved ones and make them perfect often leads to criticism. Being dissatisfied with their performance in our hearts, we put pressure on them to improve. We hope that if they do straighten out, they will be better for it and will thank us for helping.

There is such a thing as constructive criticism, but few know how to handle it. Our job is not to criticize. The Bible says the Holy Spirit is sent to "reprove the world of sin, and of righteousness, and of judgment" (John 16:8). Scripture also says that all judgment was given to Jesus, and that it is the Father's job to chastise. Our job is to speak the good news.

We are to be God's instrument in bringing a word of correction in certain instances, but we must not be the one who criticizes. The Holy Spirit must correct through us; we must not try to do His job for Him. God's correction is always redemptive and designed to restore that individual. He sets up the time and the opportunity, and He does the speaking. We must yield ourselves to the Lord at that moment. If we are humble, He may let us be the faithful instrument, and the person we are speaking to will sense that our words are from the Lord.

The Delayed Reaction

This was driven home to me one day when one of my sons was just a little boy. I discovered that he was doing something that I had repeatedly instructed him not to do. As soon as I saw his disobedience, anger rose within me. I hollered out his name, called him over, and began to chew him out with cutting words. Then I seemed to be standing outside of myself, watching my tirade against my son. I saw him withering under the attack and something hit me. I thought to myself, "I'm destroying him. This is no way to correct him."

I stopped, went in the other room, and started to pray. I asked the Lord to forgive me and show me what I was supposed to do. The Lord simply said, "Ask for a delayed reaction." I wasn't sure exactly what that would do, but that's what I prayed for. I said, "Oh, Lord, give me a delayed reaction so if I see him disobeying again I'll have time enough to pray."

When we are being taught by the Lord, He doesn't take long to drive a lesson home. Half an hour later, I saw my son doing the same thing! That same anger welled up within me, but I was able to catch it in time to offer a struggling prayer to God. I said, "God, I don't know how to handle this. You take it."

The pressure inside melted away. I called my son over, sat him down, and in a very calm tone of voice I asked, "Son what were you doing?" His head went down. "You know that it is wrong, don't you?"

With a small voice he said, "Yes."

I said, "Well, you know what I've got to do then, don't you?"

He cried a little and said, "Yes."

I said, "Son, I don't want to do it. I love you. But you have got to learn that kind of behavior is wrong." So I applied the appropriate correction to the part of the body that's made for it, and my son never did it again.

Somehow even that little boy knew the difference between my vengeance and God's justice. There's a tremendous difference between my trying to convict my son and correct him and the Holy Spirit doing it through me. I simply needed to catch myself in time and yield to the Lord and ask Him to take over. Ask for a delayed reaction.

Self-Inflicted Criticism

Self-condemnation is a powerful force that drives many insecure people to criticize others. Many people are so incapacitated by self-hatred that they are at the end of their ropes. These broken people, suffering from lives that have been torn to shreds, find it hard to love themselves or anyone else. A destructive stream of criticism flows out of them to their spouses, their children, and anyone else near them.

As I turned into my driveway one day, I watched our seven-year-old neighbor helping his father sweep their driveway. The father had swept the dirt into a pile, and the boy was holding the dust pan for him. Then very proudly, the little fellow carried the dirt over to the garbage pail. Helping his father was really a big thing for the son. He was excited.

Just as he was about to dump the dirt into the can, the dust pan caught on the lip of the garbage can and spilled dirt all over the ground. Scarcely had the dirt cascaded to the ground when the father exploded like a volcano. He came roaring down on the boy, calling him stupid and a little fool, and slapped him. The beautiful moment between the father and son was shattered, and something in the boy was destroyed. I almost wept when I saw it.

I could remember those years when I had been filled with such hatred. I had learned to be self-critical from my parents and had been passing it on to my children. By His grace God has spared my children. But I wondered how that little boy would grow up. How much hatred would be in his heart? Thinking about it was almost unbearable.

How does this destructive force of self-condemnation get inside us? Our impressions and ideas of what others think of us are major contributors to our self-image. Our parents may not have thought very much of us and others might have

put us down, but we need to live by the opinion
that the Lord has of us. How does God think of
us? How does He see us?

God Sees the End Result

One of the most remarkable passages on how
God sees His people is from the life of David. As
an old man who was approaching the end of his
life, David wrote,

> The Lord rewarded me according to my
> righteousness: according to the clean-
> ness of my hands hath he recompensed
> me. For I have kept the ways of the Lord,
> and have not wickedly departed from
> my God—2 Samuel 22:21,22.

Did you raise an eyebrow at that last statement?
Did you ask yourself, "How can this be? I know
the story. David, how can you say that? Don't you
remember the time when you committed adultery
with another man's wife? As if that wasn't bad
enough, you killed her husband to cover it up! You
didn't even repent for months."

David went on to write,

> For all his judgments were before me:
> and as for his statutes, I did not depart
> from them—2 Samuel 22:23.

Shocked by his audacity, many of us would ask, "David, don't you remember what kind of a father you were? When Absalom sinned and ran away from you, you wouldn't let him come back and see you for years. Your general, Joab, had to trick you into it. Finally, when you let Absalom come into your presence, you just gave him a peck on the cheek and sent him away. No wonder he became a rebel. David, don't you remember what kind of a father you were? How can you say those things?"

David continued,

> I was also upright before him and have kept myself from mine iniquity. Therefore the Lord hath recompensed me according to my righteousness; according to my cleanness in his eye sight—2 Samuel 22:24,25.

The Lord must have some poor eyesight!

How can David boldly pen such righteous statements about himself? Was it because David was an old man and "had his act together?" Was it because he had been doing things right for a number of years? No, because several chapters later he committed one of his worst sins—he numbered Israel against God's command, causing thousands of his people to die. No, David didn't have his act together, yet God saw him as righteous because of the great price that Jesus paid at the cross.

God was looking at David like this even during David's lifetime—not after David had died and gone to heaven. This is how God sees you and me in our lifetime. How then do you view yourself? If God is for us, how can we ever be against ourselves?

If we can put an end to our self-criticism, then a great deal of criticism toward others will also stop. Remember that our love for others is measured by our love for ourselves. (See Matthew 19:19.)

Let Them Crucify You

Any kind of criticism will eventually lead to conflicts. The Scriptures tell us that striving and disputing must not even be a part of the Christian's life. "Let nothing be done through strife or vainglory" (Philippians 2:3). Nothing! Selfish behavior is not a part of the Christian's life.

The apostle Paul reiterates, "Do *all* things without murmurings and disputings" (Philippians 2:14, italics added). These deadly weapons are not to be part of a Christian's arsenal.

You might say, "Oh, you don't know my wife. She just won't stop nagging me. She's after me all the time, picking to pieces everything I do." If you are a Christian, you are to let her crucify you if necessary. You are not to fight back, to dispute, or murmur.

If your wife or husband or someone else runs all over you in spiked shoes, let them. Somewhere, sometime, someone has got to break the vicious, strife-filled cycle; someone has to accept, has to forgive, has to allow the other even to destroy him, without destroying back.

Who will it be? Who will do it? Shouldn't God's own redeemed child be the one? Aren't we called to take up our crosses, to follow Him through the gate, out of the city, and up on that hill, to let them crucify us with Him?

We must be willing to die at the hands of another. We must do good to those who despitefully use and persecute us. We must bless those who curse us. Isn't this what it means to be a Christian? Isn't this the only way to overcome? Only these selfless actions will mold us into the image of Christ.

This is what Moses did when he stood in the gap and pleaded with God not to destroy God's people, even though these were the people that kept murmuring and complaining against him. Moses was willing to be blotted out of God's book if it would help the people.

David left us a similar example of what it means to love our enemies:

Fierce witnesses rise up; they ask me things that I do not know. They reward me evil for good, to the sorrow of my soul.

But as for me, when they were sick, my clothing was sackcloth; I humbled myself with fasting; and my prayer would return to my own heart. I paced about as though he were my friend or brother. I bowed down heavily, as one who mourns for his mother—Psalm 35:11-14, NKJV.

Sacrificing ourselves for others is a matter of our outlook, our thoughts, and our will. We must consciously determine to place a higher value on others than we place on ourselves. "In lowliness of mind let each esteem others better than himself" (Philippians 2:3, NKJV). In each circumstance you must deliberately determine to have such an attitude and outlook.

Perhaps it is a brother-in-law who antagonizes us. Maybe it is a boss who pushes us around on the job. We must decide not to criticize but rather to lift them up, even in our own mind. Sure, it is hard. We live "in the midst of a crooked and perverse generation" (Philippians 2:15). But so much more will be our glory and joy when we finally attain this mind of Christ. The key is to ask God to remind you of these truths until they are formed in you.

Caring Enough to Confront

At times you have to confront someone and show them where they've sinned. I have found a beautiful, scriptural way to do this.

First of all, invite the other person to share until they have aired all their frustrations concerning your offenses. Encourage them to tell you more; show them that you're really listening. Tell them that you want to change. Keep them talking until they've emptied their heart of what they have against you.

While they're doing so, don't defend yourself. Don't try to explain what you meant by this or why you did that. Just draw them out, looking for the incidents that are true. Discover the areas in which you really do need to repent.

When they're finally finished, honestly and fully repent of those sins you really have committed— even if they're just small offenses, like a lack of sensitivity or not seeing their hurt sooner. Be willing to confess it and repent before them.

With this approach, you will have accomplished two things. First, because you've let them talk without responding, you have in a sense earned your own right to speak. Second, because you've honestly and humbly taken the beam out of your own eye before looking at them, you've set up the atmosphere for them to repent.

After you've made peace together, simply say, "Well, there are a few things that you've done that I'd like to speak to you about." Not overstating or understating their offense, tell them exactly what they've done. With gentleness ask them to repent.

They should not just repent to make peace by saying, "I'm sorry I hurt you," and then you hug and make up. You must lead them to a repentance where they are acknowledging the truth of what they did wrong. The apostle Paul gave these instructions to Timothy:

> A servant of the Lord must not quarrel but be gentle to all, able to teach, patient, in humility correcting those who are in opposition, if God perhaps will grant them repentance, so that they may know the truth, and that they may come to their senses and escape the snare of the devil, having been taken captive by him to do his will—2 Timothy 2:24-26, NKJV.

It's important that they be fully cleansed and escape from the snare of the devil who has taken them captive to do his will. Practicing these truths will keep your heart and the hearts of others pure and clean.

What Do You See?

Developing negative patterns of thinking toward someone is another mind trap. Not being able to look at that person without thinking of their offenses can be quite a snare. This often happens between parents and a particular child. Soon all they can see is the child's failings.

I illustrated this once by taking a five-inch by eight-inch card and drawing a black spot on it about one inch in diameter. The black spot covered less than 1/40th of the card. I held up the card to a class and asked, "What do you see?"

"I see a black spot," most of them blurted out.

After thinking a little further, some began to say, "I see a white card with a black spot on it."

This happens with certain people. We most easily see the black part of another's life. Their failings may be only a small part, 1/40th, two and one-half percent, but we see them before we see the rest.

If you are caught in this kind of negative thinking, confess it before the Lord. Repent to that person and ask for their forgiveness. Then ask the Holy Spirit for an alarm system so that if such negative thinking returns, you will consciously rebuke the thoughts and drive them from your mind.

As you do this over a few weeks, those thoughts will lose their power, and your attitude toward them will become more like Christ's. If you are in the midst of a difficult relationship with another person, you *must* do this. To harbor a critical spirit will not only jeopardize your opportunity to be an overcomer, it will destroy you.

Your First Reaction

Becoming an overcomer requires more than just keeping yourself from a negative mind-set. You must develop a positive heart-set. Scripture says if any man sees his brother commit a sin that is not unto death, he should pray for him and God will give him life. (See 1 John 5:16.)

Your first reaction should be to immediately pray for your brother so God will restore him. Stand in the gap between that person and the destructive power of the sin he has committed. If you will pray for him, God will block that destructive power and give life into his spirit to help cleanse that person. We have tremendous power in our prayers.

The Scriptures teach that love beareth all things and believeth all things. (See 1 Corinthians 13:7.)

In other words, when we see someone sin, we try and explain it as best we can in their favor. This should be our first reaction until perhaps we are proven wrong.

Some may scoff, believing such thinking is naive—that you are leaving yourself open to be hurt. But reacting this way is honest and just. Even our secular government says that people are innocent until proven guilty. That is the way I want everyone to look at me.

The New Testament words for admonish, reprove, convict, and rebuke are all much lighter words than our English words. The Greek word for admonish, *noutheteo,* simply means to put in mind or remind someone. The words reprove, convict, and rebuke are all the same word in the Greek—*elegcho*—which simply means to convince. Another word for rebuke is *epitimao,* meaning to put weight upon. In other words, show a person how serious it is.

The Bible seldom speaks as sternly as we often do, especially to other Christians. At times, however, a stern rebuke is necessary. If a Christian demonstrated stubbornness or rebellion instead of repentance, the New Testament writers often addressed this by adding an adverb to the verb. For example, in Titus 1:13 Paul tells Titus to rebuke the Cretans *sharply.* Such strong admonition is reserved for serious and unrepentant acts.

Seeing the New Man

The mind-set that we ought to have toward Christian people is one that my wife pointed out to me one day when she said, "Bob, I basically look at Christians as though they're good and they don't really want to hurt anybody. At times they fall into sin because they are weak. What they need instead of rebuke is a little encouragement and a little more love. I know that at times they don't repent, and they get hardened. *Then* they need a sharp rebuke. But I don't begin by looking at them as hard and unrepentant. I first see them like I'd like to be seen."

The apostle Paul made the following statement on how we are to view our brothers and sisters:

> Therefore, from now on, we regard no one according to the flesh. Even though we have known Christ according to the flesh, yet now we know Him thus no longer.
> Therefore, if anyone is in Christ, he is a new creation; old things have passed away; behold, all things have become new—2 Corinthians 5:16,17, NKJV.

My son, whom I so harshly rebuked as a little boy, has gone on to study for the ministry. He reminded me that since we've come to Christ, we have a new spirit and have become new creatures. The old spirit or the old man is nailed to the cross with Christ. Our new man or our new spirit belongs to the Lord.

This part of redeemed man never sins and hasn't sinned since the day we came to Christ. Even though our regenerated spirits experience the pressure of the bodily and mental appetites, they don't want to fall. When the lusts of the flesh pressure our spirits to succumb, they drag their feet all the way down. Though we sin in one sense, our spirits don't. (See Romans 7:17.)

My son asked, "Dad, when we look at Christians, aren't we supposed to honor that new man and not look at them as though they're the same old person they were before Christ? Aren't we to honor their new spirit and treat them as people who don't really want to sin?" His timely word helped me to combat a critical spirit that was trying to get a foothold in my mind.

Scripture tells us that the kindness, forbearance, and longsuffering of God bring us to repentance. (See Romans 2:4.) Forbearance is one of the most remarkable concepts in Scripture. The Greek word *anóche* means not to hold a sin against somebody and not to charge it to their record. Today we might say this is "cutting them some slack."

How does Scripture encourage us to demonstrate forbearance? "The discretion of a man makes him slow to anger, and it is his glory to overlook a transgression" (Proverbs 19:11, NKJV).

Think of Stephen as he was being stoned to death. He not only refused to count their sins against them, but he was also praying life upon those who were stoning him to death when he said, "Lord, do not charge them with this sin" (Acts 7:60, NKJV).

With that kind of forbearance we can grant to others the same kind of mercy that God has extended to us. And that's exactly what He expects us to do—even in the heat of the furnace.

CHAPTER TWELVE

Sick of Sin

I was sick of my sins. After the infilling of the Spirit, I became even more conscious of the sins in my life. I came to loathe them so much that I repeatedly cried in desperation, "Lord, help me to overcome these sins! Show me how to win the battle!" As usual, He heard my prayer.

While in the midst of the problems in my congregation, our family went on a vacation to the Colorado Rockies. We packed our camper and drove high into the mountains. Hidden away from the world among towering aspens and pines, we enjoyed a weekend of camping and hiking.

Despite this beautiful time with my family, my heart was heavy. I had come on an anxious quest to seek help from the Lord in overcoming my besetting sins.

Each morning after breakfast I climbed higher into the Rockies. Near the timberline in a cleft in the rock I discovered a little quiet place to hide away. Men in the Bible must have come to similar places where the world was out of sight and almost out of mind.

With my Bible in hand, I searched and prayed for hours, crying out to God for an answer. On that mountain God began to teach me, but it was only a beginning. Over a period of months the answer slowly unfolded. God's revelation on overcoming besetting sins came to me experientially—the slow, hard way—but it did come.

Walk in the Spirit

The secret of overcoming, I discovered, was to *"walk in the Spirit"* (Galatians 5:16). Although I had been baptized with the Spirit for many years, it was only then that I began to grasp what it meant to walk in the Spirit.

The Scriptures make some tremendous promises to those who apply this spiritual principle.

> There is therefore now no condemnation to them which are in Christ Jesus, who walk not after the flesh, but after the Spirit—Romans 8:1.

No matter what rod you measure yourself by, no matter what standard you set for yourself, no matter what people think of you, you will come under no condemnation if you are walking in the Spirit and not in the flesh.

The apostle Paul's letter continues,

> That the righteousness of the law might
> be fulfilled in us, who walk not after the
> flesh, but after the Spirit—Romans 8:4.

The righteousness of the law is so perfect that no one except Jesus has even come close to living it.

God's commands and statutes are so perfect and beautiful and good. For many years I had lamented, "If only I could live that way." Then I saw it. God's answer to holy, righteous living was to walk in the Spirit.

If we are spiritually minded, God's Word also promises us life and peace. (See Romans 8:6.) As we walk in the Spirit and think in the Spirit, God's very life will come into our hearts and minds. The very One who shapes and creates will fill our steps, and we will overcome and find the peace that only God can give.

I gradually learned the lesson of walking in the Spirit over a long period of time. Insight came in bits and pieces—sort of hit and miss—but I will try to present it in a more orderly fashion.

On a Journey

Let us start with the word *walk*. In Greek, the original language of the New Testament, there are three main words for walk. The first is clearly seen in the following passage:

> Then had the churches rest throughout all Judea and Galilee and Samaria, and were edified; and *walking* in the fear of the Lord, and in the comfort of the Holy Ghost, were multiplied—Acts 9:31, italics added.

The Greek word for walk here is *poreuomai,* which simply means "to pass through," "to go from one point to another," or "to journey," referring to our total walk. We are to set out on a journey with the Lord.

Part of walking in the Spirit is to commit ourselves to that journey with the Lord. Without that first initial commitment, we will flounder again and again. We will be blown about by other winds that send us careening in different directions. If that happens, we will only have to come back and start over. From the beginning we must decide which direction we are going and whose journey we are on. Will we follow Jesus or be led about by our own whims?

Remember, we cannot go in two directions. Many people surrender themselves to Jesus but not fully. While they say they would like to walk with Him, their hearts are divided. Because they aren't totally surrendered to the Lord, they never overcome their besetting sins.

A Divided Heart

The problem of a divided heart affected the people of Israel and caused them to sin time and time again. When Moses was up on the mountain, the people came to Aaron, the high priest, and said, "Make us a god to take us back to Egypt. We were better off there than we are out in this wilderness."

Aaron refused for a time, but the Israelites pressed him so that he finally yielded and said, "Give me your earrings of gold." Aaron took them, melted them down, and formed a golden calf. He said, "Here O Israel is your god to bring you back to Egypt." But then he said something to the effect, "Today we worship the golden calf, but tomorrow we worship Jehovah." (See Exodus 32:1-4.)

You see, Aaron and the Israelites didn't want to give up Jehovah. They all knew what God had done to the Egyptians, but they couldn't forget the pleasures of Egypt.

During the years of the kings, Israel continually struggled with a divided heart. Elijah called all the people of northern Israel to Mount Carmel and demanded that they make up their mind. He said, "How long will you falter between two opinions? If the Lord is God, follow Him; but if Baal, then follow him" (1 Kings 18:21, NKJV). But the people did not respond to Elijah's challenge.

Elijah suggested that the four hundred and fifty prophets of Baal sacrifice a bull but put no fire under it; Elijah would do the same. Then Elijah said, "Then you call on the name of your gods, and I will call on the name of the Lord; and the God who answers by fire, He is God" (1 Kings 18:24, NKJV). This found favor with the people.

So the prophets of Baal sacrificed their bull and laid it on the wood. All day long they cried out, "Baal, hear us! Baal, hear us!" Their attempts to call down fire from Baal were futile. Elijah laughed because he knew that Baal was a product of man's imagination.

At the time of the evening sacrifice, Elijah rebuilt the altar, drenched the sacrifice in water, and offered a simple prayer. The fire of God fell from heaven, consuming the sacrifice and licking up the water that Elijah had poured over the sacrifice. The people knew that day who their God was, and they helped Elijah slay the four hundred and fifty prophets of Baal. (See 1 Kings 18:26-40.)

Making Up Your Mind

We can never become overcomers if we don't have singleness of heart toward God. Through one of His prophets the Lord said, "I have declared and I have saved and I have proclaimed, and there was no foreign god among you" (Isaiah 43:12, NKJV).

In other words, when Israel worshiped God alone, He declared Himself to them and showed them His truths and His word. As a result, they grew strong. When Israel's heart was undivided, God revealed Himself and saved them from their enemies and their problems.

Have there been times in your life when you sought God with your whole heart? With singleness of mind were you compelled to seek Him for answers? Wasn't it then that He showed Himself to you, touched your life, and brought deliverance? When we have a single heart toward God, He always answers with power.

The night Jesus came walking on the water toward the disciples' boat, He was looking for an undivided heart. (See Matthew 14:22-33.) As Jesus drew near the disciples became afraid, but Jesus reassured them of His identity. Then Peter called out, "Lord, if it is You, command me to come to You on the water." Jesus said one word, "Come."

With that one word Peter stepped out of the boat onto the water and walked with joy toward Jesus. But then he looked at the waves; perhaps he took just a little glance at first. Perhaps some spray hit his face. Little by little he became more aware of the waves, the clouds, and the wind.

Then he began to sink. When he called desperately to Jesus, the Master reached out to Peter. After helping Peter into the boat, Jesus asked, "O you of little faith, why did you doubt?"

The Greek word for *doubt* is very significant. *Distazo,* which is only used twice in the Bible, means "to stand divided." Jesus asked Peter, "Why did you stand divided?" Peter hadn't stopped looking at Jesus, and he hadn't stopped trying to get closer to Him. His downfall was that he also had one eye on the storm.

When we have a divided heart, we will sink. We will lose the miraculous touch on our lives, and Jesus will have to pull us out of the mess we got ourselves into. We cannot be overcomers if we have a divided heart. If we have not decided that our lives are to be lived for Him, we will never enjoy the power of victorious lives. We must deliberately set out on His journey.

Three Kinds of Repentance

Aside from earnest prayer, how does one acquire an undivided heart toward the Lord? How do we obtain total surrender, and how can we stay on His journey? There is one essential factor. You must have honest, old-fashioned repentance.

There are basically three kinds of repentance in the Bible. Let's look at three different men who said the words, "I have sinned." Each one, however, had a different motive.

First, there was Pharaoh. When the plagues of God came crashing down upon Egypt, Pharaoh called for Moses and said, "I have sinned this time: the Lord is righteous, and I and my people are wicked" (Exodus 9:27). Those words were very true. But his repentance was motivated from pressure to get out from under the problem. Pharaoh's heart was not broken. As soon as the plague stopped and the pressure was off, he hardened his heart.

Let's examine the repentance of another man who cried out, "I have sinned." Judas betrayed the Lord, saw the enormity of his sin, returned to the priests with whom he had made his loathsome bargain, and confessed, "I have sinned by betraying innocent blood" (Matthew 27:4, NKJV).

The priests sneered at Judas. The world has no pity when you fall into sin. The priests replied, "What is that to us? You see to it!" Their merciless response was more than Judas could bear. Overwhelmed by his sin, he threw the money at their feet and went out and hung himself. (See Matthew 27:5,6.)

Unlike Pharaoh, Judas' repentance was not from outward pressure but inward pressure. Judas repented because he realized he was not the man he thought he was. He was a failure. His repentance was born out of self-pity. Notice that Judas did not go back to the One he had wronged to confess, "Oh, Lord, I am sorry I have sinned against You; please forgive me." No, he didn't even think of that. He could only think of himself. Judas had not failed Christ as much as he had failed Judas.

Many Christians have a repentance of self-pity. They think they are sorry. They say the right words, but they are blind to the hurt they have inflicted on God and those around them. Their remorse is not linked to action. They do not go to those they have hurt and ask forgiveness; they are simply sorry that they are such failures. Remorse is not enough.

The third example of repentance in the Scriptures involves the prodigal son. After he took his inheritance, left home, and wasted the money on riotous living, a great famine occurred in the land, leaving him with nothing to eat. When he finally realized the foolishness of his actions, he said, "How many hired servants of my father's have bread enough and to spare, and I perish with hunger! I will arise and go to my father, and will say to him, 'Father, I have sinned against heaven and before you and I am no longer worthy to be called your son. Make me like one of your hired servants' " (Luke 15:17-19, NKJV).

Even though he wanted to get out from under the pressure, and perhaps he experienced some self-pity, yet the prodigal's repentance went far deeper than that. He knew that his rebellion had shamed his God and his father. His repentance led the prodigal son to return, humble himself, and seek restoration with his father.

This is the kind of response that God desires to bless. True repentance leads to a full surrender and an undivided heart. "A broken and a contrite heart—these, O God, You will not despise" (Psalm 51:17, NKJV).

So the first step in walking in the Spirit is to honestly repent and to set out to go all the way in the Lord's journey. We must deliberately determine to walk by His side no matter what the consequences—even if we must die for it. This is *poreuomai*—walking His walk.

Step by Step Obedience

To overcome we must also understand the principles behind the two other words for *walk*. They are both found in the fifth chapter of Galatians. The first is: "*Walk* in the Spirit, and you shall not fulfill the lust of the flesh" (Galatians 5:16).

In this verse the Greek word for walk has an entirely different meaning. *Peripateo* refers to habitual conduct, or a step by step walking. In addition to committing ourselves to the entire journey, we need to take one step at a time to arrive at our destination. We should not just pray, "Oh, God, I will be faithful the rest of my life," for God will ask, "Yes, but how about this afternoon?" or "How about this evening?"

What about how much we eat for supper or what we watch on TV or how late we get to bed? We are to take each circumstance item by item and determine to do that particular task God's way. Consciously, by an act of our will, we must determine to take that next correct step in the Lord. Remember that our walk with the Lord is also an ongoing, step by step surrender.

The apostle Paul also wrote, "If we live in the Spirit, let us also *walk* in the Spirit" (Galatians 5:25). This third distinct word for walk is *stoicheo,* meaning "to be in rank with" or "to line up with." We are to line up our lives with the Holy Spirit.

For instance, if an unedifying magazine or book is in the house, we must get rid of it. Perhaps we have friends that we know are not good for us. Oh, we can witness to them, but the Spirit may say not to walk with them. Perhaps we must sever or add something to our life in order to stay faithful to the Lord. God says that no matter how hard it is, make that decision and do it.

God may direct us to give up a certain pleasure or hobby that He has not asked others to forsake.

That's all right. Give it up anyway. Some activities are not sinful in themselves, but if they get out of control He may say, "If your right eye causes you to sin, pluck it out and cast it from you" (Matthew 5:29, NKJV). Some activities may not be sin in themselves; they may even be fine for other people, but if they lead you to sin, get rid of them. You must deal decisively with anything that might be a snare. In all areas our lives must line up with the Spirit.

The Missing Piece

You may be saying, "That sounds great, but there must be something more to it. I've surrendered myself to the Lord, and as much as it lies with me, I've tried to have singleness of heart. I've tried to take it an item at a time. And I know that I've tried to line up my life properly. And still, I habitually fall into sin. I repeatedly fail the Lord. A piece of the puzzle must be missing."

The final ingredient for overcoming was, to me, the greatest liberation of all. I began to see it while I was on that mountain top in Colorado. The puzzle pieces of how to be an overcomer began to fall into place as I read the epistles.

The apostle Paul in Colossians 1:25-27 describes a mystery that God had concealed from the very beginning of time. Throughout the Old Testament

God's people lived and died, yet they had no revelation of one of God's greatest secrets. But now the mystery has been made known among the Gentiles, which is *"Christ in you,* the hope of glory" (Colossians 1:27).

This whole concept of Christ in us began to blossom in me. I saw it again and again as I read Scripture.

> Christ is all, and in all—Colossians 3:11.

> I have been crucified with Christ; it is no longer I who live, but Christ lives in me; and the life which I now live in the flesh I live by faith in the Son of God, who loved me and gave Himself for me—Galatians 2:20, NKJV.

> My little children, for whom I labor in birth again until Christ is formed in you—Galatians 4:19, NKJV.

> But we have this treasure in earthen vessels, that the excellence of the power may be of God and not of us—2 Corinthians 4:7, NKJV.

> I in them, and You in Me; that they may be made perfect in one—John 17:23, NKJV.

> If Christ be in you, the body is dead
> because of sin; but the Spirit is life
> because of righteousness—Romans 8:10.

Again and again in Scripture I saw this principle. At first I thought it was just some nice saying about Christ being near us and being interested in our lives. But it's far more than that. Scripture repeatedly affirms that Christ is in me, living through me. What a miracle!

It's Not What We Do

Finally the Lord coupled the concept of the indwelling Christ with the key of yielding to God. The apostle Paul says the overcoming life is not a matter of something we are to do or not to do. Such is the relationship of being under the Law. Instead we live under grace, which puts the requirements upon Jesus Christ. Grace says He does it all for us and hands it to us as a gift. (See Romans 6:12-14.)

This is how we were saved in the first place. Salvation involves nothing that we did. We are not going to heaven because we were nice to our neighbor when she was ill or helped mow a buddy's lawn when he was disabled.

We are going to heaven solely because of what Christ did for us. That's grace—a free gift from

Him. We do not walk before God from day to day by our righteousness, but we walk under grace. Jesus does it for us. He doesn't just help us. Jesus conquers each temptation through us. He accomplishes every deed in our lives, for He is in us, not just with us.

Walking in the Spirit is primarily a matter of *yielding*. Romans 6:13 says to "*yield* yourselves unto God . . . and your members as instruments of righteousness unto God." Yield your attitudes, your feelings, your body, your mind, your will, and your spirit.

You will come under the reigning power of Jesus in every item that you yield to Him. Jesus' power will begin to rule your life in this situation because He is in you and will take over as you yield to Him. He will drive away the temptation.

All of us have felt the gripping, ruling power of sin. But Jesus is stronger than sin. He has conquered sin and will conquer it in us if we let Him. Who wins the war on your moral battlegrounds? The outcome is determined by whose rulership we yield to.

This is the great difference between the Old and New Testaments. In the Old Testament men were trying by their own strength to live righteously before God. In the New Testament men are living by the power of Christ that works through them.

This is what the apostle Paul meant when he wrote "for me to live is Christ" (Philippians 1:21).

Doomed to Fail

To give a practical illustration of how this works, let me first describe the Old Testament way of sanctification under the Law.

Suppose you have just enjoyed a marvelous Thanksgiving dinner. Feeling absolutely stuffed, you may say to yourself, "Well, there is a time for feasting, and there is a time for fasting. I am not going to eat any more tonight. I have had plenty."

You may even promise the Lord that you will eat nothing else. Such promises are easy to make right after the meal. But what happens about nine o'clock that evening while you are watching television? A mouth-watering pizza appears on a commercial, and your taste buds are tantalized with a description of each delicious ingredient. In your mind flashes one word: "pizza." You drive it from your mind. You say, "No, I am not going to eat. I promised."

The movie is on again, but in a few minutes another commercial appears. This time whipped dessert topping is advertised. Look how they spread it on pumpkin pie. You think, "Boy, that looks good." But you catch yourself. You have had plenty to eat. You may even ask the Lord for help.

(When we ask the Lord to help, He will, but He wants us to ask for more than help. He wants to teach us a better way.)

You think, "There is one piece of pumpkin pie left. My, that would be good with some topping. No, no, I will not do it." At last the movie is on again. Soon another food commercial interrupts. Your mind goes blank. With a glazed look in your eyes you get up from the couch and head toward the refrigerator. Oh, no! There are two pieces of pumpkin pie left. You thought if there was only one you might as well finish it off. Oh well, you take a piece.

As you return to your seat the movie is back on. You don't dare think about what you are doing. You gobble down the piece of pie twice as fast as you usually would because you are already feeling guilty.

Just as you take the last bite, the demonic accuser, who helped prod you to eat in the first place, now whispers, "You've done it again, you sinner. You promised God you would not eat any more tonight. What a failure!"

You moan and groan and cry, "Oh, God, why am I such a failure? Why can't I control myself?" And you plead with the Lord to forgive you. You agonize for a while until you have appeased your conscience somewhat.

This is a far worse sin than having eaten the pie because you are beating yourself instead of trusting the beating that Jesus took at Calvary as payment for your sin. We should just go humbly to the Lord and admit our sin and how we have hurt Him and ask His forgiveness. Then we should get up and go on, knowing that the blood of Jesus covers our sin and that God never again calls our transgression to mind.

If you don't seek God's forgiveness, you will seek to escape from your guilt. You may feel so bad that you go back for the last piece of pie just to drown your feelings of condemnation.

Have you ever been down that road, my friend? Have you gritted your teeth in determination— only to quickly fall? Have you gathered your willpower, set your jaw, planted your feet firmly, and solemnly sworn, "God, I will not do that again," only to do that exact thing an hour and a half later? That is a terrible road to travel.

Walking by Grace

The Old Testament method of sanctification required men to cleanse themselves with their own efforts and will power. No wonder Israel could not make it. But God has a new plan, a new covenant, and a New Testament. Those who belong to Jesus live under that new covenant. What does it mean to live under grace?

Suppose this time you have just finished a marvelous Christmas dinner. Once again you have stuffed yourself. You tenderly pat your stomach and say, "Boy, I really packed it in tonight. I will have nothing else to eat. That's enough for me."

Then you add, "Oh, oh, I remember what I did at Thanksgiving. But I will not do that again. I failed that night. But I will not fail tonight. I am not going to stand in my own strength. Lord, I am not asking You for help. I am asking for more. I am asking that You take over.

"Lord, You and I both know I should not eat any more. And so I *yield* myself to You like Romans chapter six says. I yield to You my members. I yield my stomach and whatever goes on there that makes me want to eat. I yield to You my thoughts about food. I yield to You my feelings and my desires. I yield to You all the food in the house. I yield my spirit so You can intertwine my heart with Yours and keep me close to You. Fill my soul with Your presence and cleanse every unruly appetite. Jesus, You work Your will in me."

Later after you have been watching television again that night and the evening news is over, you yawn and say, "Well, honey, I guess it's time for bed." Suddenly you stop. You remember that you have eaten nothing since supper. You didn't even think about eating. Praise the Lord! Victory! But who gets the credit? Jesus does because "it is God which worketh in you both to will and to do of his good pleasure" (Philippians 2:13). Your job is to simply and honestly yield to God.

That's what it means to live under grace and let Jesus work in you. You have victory even over pumpkin pie. But not you, Christ in you. If you focus on Jesus with an undivided heart, you will be on your way to overcoming besetting sins. As you yield again and again, item by item, you will walk in the Spirit with victory.

CHAPTER THIRTEEN

Learning to Relax in the Lord

Many people are busy rushing around, working here, and running there. Most of our activities are justified, but we can overdo it until Jesus becomes squeezed out of our lives. One of the enemy's main methods of attack is to get us too busy. We can even become too busy serving the Lord!

Remember the story of Mary and Martha? (See Luke 10:38-42.) I can just see Martha getting the word that the Lord was coming to supper. If I knew that Jesus was coming to my house, I'm sure we would be in a frenzy trying to get everything ready. I imagine this is just what Martha was doing. She made sure the house was immaculate, washed all the best Kosher dinnerware, and went to the market and bought the lamb. There were a hundred things to do.

I can just see Martha answering the door and saying, "Oh, Jesus, how wonderful to see You! Come in and make Yourself at home. I will be right with You." She scurried back to the kitchen to finish preparing the meal. Wondering where her sister was, Martha peered into the parlor and glared at Mary, who was sitting on the floor at Jesus' feet, just listening to Him. Can't you sympathize with Martha as she asked, "Lord, do you not care that my sister has left me to serve alone?" (Luke 10:40, NKJV).

I can imagine the sigh of Jesus' heart as He said,

> "Martha, Martha, you are worried and troubled about many things. But one thing is needed, and Mary has chosen that good part, which will not be taken away from her"—Luke 10:41,42, NKJV.

What Jesus was really saying to Martha was, "Don't you realize that I would rather have *you* than your lamb? Getting to know Me and being My friend is more important than making sure everything is just right." Yes, it *is* more important to commune with Jesus in our prayer closet and our Bible study than to labor for Him.

The holy of holies in the Jewish temple was the inner sanctuary where the presence of God dwelt. So also, the holy of holies of our time are those moments when we are hidden away with God. The rest of the temple was the place of sacrifice and service for the Lord. This corresponds to our time of service for Him. The *focal point* of our lives that empowers us is our *time* with Him—not our serving Him.

Waiting for Ministry

Many people want to serve God. After coming to know the Lord, young believers receive the Holy Spirit and are excited to get underway in a ministry, yet they wonder why no avenue of ministry opens for them. They do not realize that first they must learn to be still and enjoy the friendship of God. Sometimes this takes years. Moses spent forty years in the wilderness of Midian tending the flocks of Jethro and getting to know God before he led the Israelites out of Egypt.

John the Baptist may have been anxious in his youth to begin his ministry. God held him back in the wilderness until He was ready to show him to Israel. When John was thirty years old, God told him to preach to the Israelites. John's close communion with God endowed him with the power and Spirit of God. Even though his ministry was only nine months long and the Bible records no great miracle done by John the Baptist, thousands repented when he preached. He prepared Israel for the coming of the Lord!

We must grasp the importance of knowing the Lord. God can do more in nine months with a man who has sat at His feet than He can in forty years

with a man who only knows Him to a limited
degree. Spend time with the Lord. Carve out the
time and dedicate it to the Lord, even if your
ministry seemingly suffers. "Delight yourself also
in the Lord, and He shall give you the desires of
your heart" (Psalm 37:4, NKJV). God will fulfill
even your ministry desires.

Remember three important truths. First, the
Lord will accomplish His work no matter what.
Second, the Lord wants to use you in getting that
work done. Third, if you are a yielded vessel, God
will indeed use you.

Peace in Performance

In ministry remember that you're not working
for the Lord, but He is working *through* you as
a yielded vessel. That's what the apostle Paul
meant in the following passages:

> For me to live is Christ—Philippians
> 1:21.

> I have been crucified with Christ; it is
> no longer I who live, but Christ lives in
> me; and the life which I now live in the
> flesh I live by faith in the Son of God,
> who loved me and gave Himself for
> me—Galatians 2:20, NKJV.

Jesus, who has called you into the ministry, will also do it through you. "He who calls you is faithful, who also will do it" (1 Thessalonians 5:24, NKJV). The apostle Paul wrote, "It is God which worketh in you both to will and to do of his good pleasure" (Philippians 2:13).

If this is the case, then don't get discouraged if your ministry doesn't seem to be taking off. Your job is not to produce for Him but to allow Him to produce through you. You will be judged by how yielded a vessel you were—not by how much you accomplished.

You are not in competition with others who seem to have great, flourishing ministries and are well known all over the world. They have only twenty-four hours in a day, just as you have. The same Lord who works through them also works through you. Anything that is accomplished for the kingdom of God is done by Him, so there is no room for envy. The Lord is looking for faithful and obedient sons and daughters.

That's why the apostle Paul wrote,

> God hath tempered the body together, having given more abundant honour to that part which lacked: that there should be no schism in the body; but that the members should have the same care one for another—1 Corinthians 12:24,25.

God will by undeserved grace give more abundant honor to those parts of the body that are lacking in natural talent and ability.

Why does God do that? So there will be no division in the Body of Christ. God wants the members of the Body to have the same concern and regard for you that they have for Moses, Paul, or David.

You don't need to be jealous or cast down. Comparing yourself with others or being critical of yourself doesn't help. God will graciously add more abundant honor to you if you lack. Moses, David, Luther, and every great man or woman of God received their honor by grace, too. Christ is everything. "Ye are dead, and your life is hid with Christ in God" (Colossians 3:3). That's why, if we are yielded, we can be at peace in the Lord and not be overly concerned with our performance.

A Heavy Burden?

While speaking at my first large Christian conference, I discovered another area of my life that needed God's attention. I was one of three speakers. Twelve hundred people packed our first evening service, and I was excited for the opportunity to speak to such a crowd.

Since receiving my call into the ministry, I knew I was not meant to be a pastor. Shepherding the flock is a hard, exacting, in-depth ministry. I knew my call had a broader base that would take me to many people.

Finally, after many years of pastoring, I was addressing my first large group of people. I felt like an eagle soaring. That night I preached my heart out. It was beautiful. The next morning I was on deck for the first of the morning sessions, and again I gave it all I had. I was smiling so much from ear to ear that the back of my jaw ached. I was bursting for joy.

During the break between the two morning sessions, a lady with a very serious expression came up to me. I thought she must be carrying some heavy burden. She asked, "Pastor Heil, could I speak to you for a moment?"

"Sure," I answered.

"Could we go over to the side away from the others and pull up some chairs for a few minutes? This is very important."

I nodded. We found some chairs and prayed. Then she spoke.

"I hardly know where to begin. I guess it all started about a month ago when I was praying. I had a vision of you. I could see your face and under your face your name was spelled out.

"I had no idea what it meant, until about a week ago. Your picture came on television with your name spelled out under it exactly as I had seen it in the vision. You were to be one of the speakers at this conference. Still I did not know what it meant.

"Then, last night after the service, I went home and began to pray for you. The Lord gave me some Bible passages. Here, these are for you," she opened her purse and pulled out a list of Scriptures.

"Especially the passage in Isaiah 61. God wants to take the robe of righteousness and just snuggle you up tight in it." (She reached out at me, took an imaginary robe, and pretended to wrap it around me and pull it tight.) "He wants to do that until some terrible burden that is upon you is gone."

There was a pause as she looked at me. "You look so happy and you've been smiling so much, yet there is some burden upon you that is crushing and breaking you. God wants to remove it. It has something to do with the robe of righteousness, but I do not know exactly what it means."

Well, by this time my defenses were up, and I was taking all this with a huge grain of salt. Surely there must be a passage somewhere stating that many kooks will go out into the world in the name of Jesus. Obviously, she was one of them. I had no burden crushing and breaking me, but I decided to check it out. I've thanked God many times that

I did because I learned one of the greatest lessons of my life.

My first check point is always, "Is it scriptural?" Well, in this case it was hard to be more scriptural for these were Bible passages she had given me. My second check point is, "What's the internal witness in my heart?" I had yes and no going at the same time. I didn't know what to make of it. My third check point is, "How does it fit the circumstances of my life?" Is it something right on target or way off in left field?

I thought this woman was way off base. I certainly was happy—so happy I couldn't even stop smiling as she told me all this. When she finished I was still grinning from ear to ear. I didn't know of any burden crushing my life.

Even though I gave her remarks a great big negative check mark, I still couldn't throw them out. Something inside made me go through a fourth major checkpoint, "What's the testimony of the brethren about her personally?" Thinking she might be some sort of unbalanced religious nut, I decided to check her out. I asked this woman what church she attended and who her pastor was.

Later that day I called her pastor and asked, "Do you know Sister So-and-So?"

"Yes, she is a member of my congregation. Why do you ask?"

"What kind of woman is she? Is she given to flights of spiritual fancy and religious day-dreaming?"

"No, she is a solid Christian woman. She has her feet right on the ground. Why? Did she give you some Bible passages?"

I gulped and said, "Yes, she did."

"Well, that has happened several times before, and each time she has been right on target. I would pay attention to those Scriptures if I were you," the pastor admonished me.

I thanked him and took another look at the passages. I prayed over them. Still I couldn't understand what God was trying to say. I didn't have any crushing burden. Nothing was breaking me. I put the passages away and figured God would give me insight at some later date.

The Robe of Righteousness

That night, after the large evening meeting, I was ministering with some people. I had just finished praying with a man to receive the baptism of the Holy Spirit when I turned around and saw a large woman with white hair, white shoes, and a big white purse. As she approached me, she pulled a big white envelope out of her purse and said, "Pastor, this is for you."

I thought, "Oh, a special offering."

But she said, "These are some Bible passages that the Lord directed me to give to you."

I paused, "Really! Who is your pastor?"

I checked with him. This woman's story was similar to the first lady who gave me Scripture earlier in the day. Her pastor said she was a fine Christian woman who knows the mind of the Lord. I looked at the passages. They dove-tailed with the first set.

This was no mere coincidence. My mind was reeling. There was only one thing to do: seek the help of the elders of the conference. I called the host pastor and the other two speakers, and they met me in my motel room. I told them what had happened and began to read the Scripture verses. As I was about to read the Isaiah 61:10 passage, the host pastor stopped me.

"Bob, don't you see it? That's what I've been trying to tell you all day. I did not know exactly what, but I knew God was trying to say something to you through me. Don't you understand?"

Puzzled and perplexed, I shook my head. I read the scripture, "I will greatly rejoice in the Lord, my soul shall be joyful in my God; for he hath clothed me with the garments of salvation, he hath covered me with the robe of righteousness, as a bridegroom decketh himself with ornaments, and as a bride adorneth herself with her jewels."

Ever since I had knelt in that little machine shop in Kansas, I knew I was saved. I have never had a moment's doubt. I knew no matter how great my sin, Jesus had already paid for it. I had the "garment of salvation." But I thought the "robe of righteousness" was the same thing as the "garment of salvation." Now I began to see that it was more.

Suddenly a veil lifted from my eyes. The Spirit fell on me more suddenly and dramatically than when I was baptized in the Holy Spirit. I fell to my knees. My heart jumped and pounded within my chest. Tears filled my eyes, and I began to weep great, heaving sobs.

God was wrapping me in the robe of righteousness and was lifting from my shoulders the burden that had indeed been crushing and destroying me. I had lived with this burden for so long that I had grown accustomed to it. I thought it was normal to live this way. The weight that had robbed me of peace and joy began to lift as God spoke to me there on my knees.

He said, "My son, I have not only given you the garment of salvation, but you are also robed in righteousness. It is my gift to you. I adorn you with it as a bridegroom is adorned. My son, *stop beating yourself.* My responsibility is to make you righteous. You cannot add to the beating I endured at the cross. I took it all. You must forgive yourself." He went on, "Bob who is your master?"

"You are, Lord," I sobbed.

"Are you sure? Are you sure you are not your own master?"

"No, Jesus, You are my master."

"Remember the passage that admonishes you not to judge another man's servant? That in the eyes of his own master he stands or falls? I am your master; I am the only one who can beat you. And if I am not beating you, then stop beating yourself."

God's Job

Many people punish themselves almost incessantly. They downgrade themselves, dislike themselves, and are always focused on their sins. Those who condemn themselves in a thousand little ways think that such driving and pushing helps them to overcome. But Jesus took all the punishment that was needed—more than enough. In fact, when we beat ourselves we're saying that we don't fully trust the beating Christ took on the cross.

Why had I not seen this before? Why had I been so hard on myself? Why did I belittle myself so? Then the Lord added something else that really blessed me.

"My son, you are right on schedule. Because you have handed me your sins and failings, I have always turned them around 180 degrees and made blessings out of them. I will spend the rest of your life cleaning you up, and even then you will not be perfect. But it is up to Me to do that, not you. You just continue to yield to Me.''

Immediately this scripture shot into my mind: ''If we confess our sins, he is faithful and just to forgive us our sins, and to *cleanse us from all unrighteousness*'' (1 John 1:9, italics added). It's God's job to clean up our lives—not ours. All we have to do is to surrender everything to Him and be obedient to what He sets before us. He will then fulfill it. I could relax! My life was being taken care of. Oh, the joy! I thought I was happy before, but this was ecstasy. For months I floated with joy.

Eventually, though, the little self-condemning thoughts began to slip back in. Little by little I took on the old burden until finally I was again under heavy bondage.

Then one afternoon I was preparing a Bible lesson that I was to give that night, and I came across Psalm 25:15: ''Mine eyes are ever toward the Lord; for he shall pluck my feet out of the net.''

Then the still small voice of God whispered, ''Bob, where are your eyes?''

''Lord, they are on You.''

''Are you sure they are not on the net, on all the problems you get tangled in?''

''No, Lord, they are on You. I hand my problems to You.''

"Are you sure they are not looking toward your feet that keep getting caught in the net?"

I stopped and looked down. "Oh, my stupid feet!" I sighed. "Yes, God, You are right. I have been engrossed in my sins and weaknesses instead of You."

My eyes were so focused on my clumsy feet that they were not on Jesus any more. My distractions had become idolatry. Bob and his weaknesses had filled the whole horizon of my vision. Jesus said if I kept my eyes on Him, He would pluck my stumbling feet out of any net.

I repented and once again wept for joy as the lesson was driven home.

Forgiving Myself

I walked in my new-found joy for only a few months. How slow we are to really learn. Gradually my eyes began to turn inward again. Have I repented enough? Do I pray earnestly enough? Do I raise my hands high enough? Am I a good enough speaker? Why did I do this? Why didn't I do that?

In the midst of my morbid self-examination, I received a telephone call from the president of a Full Gospel Business Men's chapter. He said, "Bob, we need your help. We want you to come on a three-day retreat with the officers and leaders of our chapter. We have been having some quarrels and disagreements among ourselves, and we know this is no way to act. Can you help us?''

I said, ''Sure, I would be glad to.'' A week later I found myself in a little cabin by the Lake of the Ozarks. On the second morning I had an idea. After devotions I said, ''Men, I want you to take a piece of paper and a pencil and go to a part of the cabin where you can be alone. Write down every sin and failure that has been bugging you and then go before God this day and officially forgive *yourself* sin by sin as you know Jesus has already forgiven you. Cross off each sin so you can't read it any more, and let it be gone forever. Go down the list until you are free from all the guilt that has been condemning you.''

Off they went, and I was left alone in the large room next to the fireplace. As I sat there thinking, it dawned on me that I had never done that myself. I couldn't ignore the thought. If I had asked *them* to do it, I had better give it a try.

I got some paper and a pencil and began to write down every sin and every failure. I flipped the page over and began to fill the other side. I got a second piece of paper and then a third. I was half way through the third sheet of paper before the flood finally stopped.

You can imagine the mental and emotional energy we expend trying to keep so much garbage submerged in our subconscious. If we do not deal with our sins promptly, we may push them to the back of our minds; but they are still there under the surface. They must be dealt with decisively and officially or we will never be able to relax and find the Lord's peace.

I took my sins and failures to God one by one and dealt with them for the last time. When I had finished nearly two hours later, a whole evil root system had been dug out of me. I was free. My greatest enemy, myself, had been slain.

From that day forward, the furnace seemed not a furnace at all. The fire still raged as hot as ever in many ways, but I had a relaxing peace beyond anything I could have imagined. And beyond that, in this atmosphere of peace, my overcoming took a giant leap forward.

CHAPTER FOURTEEN

Warriors Not Weepers

Our church continued to be a hot bed of conflict. For those of us determined to hang on, the flames grew hotter. Although we were learning many lessons in God's furnace, there were times when we grew weary and almost fainted. Moments came when we felt out of tune with God, and we almost wanted to give up. Our enemies kept attacking us so furiously that God seemed a long way off.

At one point, when the fire was a long, drawn-out slow burn, we groaned and cried out to God in childish, begging terms that became the voice of doubt and complaining. In the midst of all of this noise, the Lord spoke a sovereign word to us: "I want warriors not weepers!"

The Lord reminded us that he was never far from any of His children. (See Acts 17:27.) He encouraged us to pray like warriors and break through in the heavenlies. Instead of growing weary and becoming weepers, we could be transformed into warriors by yielding to Him.

He reminded us that "the effective, fervent prayer of a righteous man avails much" (James 5:16, NKJV). "You will seek Me and find Me, when you search for Me with all your heart" (Jeremiah 29:13, NKJV).

One passage had special meaning for us. "In the days of His flesh, when He [Jesus] had offered up prayers and supplications, with vehement cries and tears to Him who was able to save Him from death, and was heard because of His godly fear" (Hebrews 5:7, NKJV).

The word used for godly fear, however, is not necessarily a good translation. This Greek word is derived from *eulabes,* which literally means to grasp or take hold of firmly. In other words, Jesus knew how to take hold of His Father's heart. He knew how to touch the Father with the fervency of His prayers. That's what God wanted us to do.

Set Yourself to Seek the Lord

By His Spirit God gradually showed us how to do this. First of all, we saw that we couldn't just pray the way we had at other times. We had to set ourselves to seek the Lord.

When David was preparing to gather all the materials to build the temple, he first set the people's heart. He charged the Israelites, "Now set your heart and your soul to seek the Lord your God" (1 Chronicles 22:19).

When Jehoshaphat discovered three mighty armies were approaching to destroy him, "Jehoshaphat feared, and set himself to seek the Lord, and proclaimed a fast throughout all Judah. So Judah gathered together to ask help from the Lord; and from all the cities of Judah they came to seek the Lord" (2 Chronicles 20:3,4, NKJV). The people of Judah didn't just add this new crisis to their prayer list. They didn't just pray around the dinner table. They took extraordinary steps to come before the Lord. Special directives meant going to Jerusalem and gathering as one mighty voice before God and before His temple.

Jesus also knew how to seek the Lord. That's why the gospels record, "When he [Jesus] had sent the multitudes away, he went up into a mountain apart to pray" (Matthew 14:23), and "In the morning, rising up a great while before day, he went out, and departed into a solitary place, and there prayed" (Mark 1:35). Jesus took specific steps to be apart with the Father.

We, too, realized that we needed—both individually and corporately—to have special times to seek the Lord. Psalm 46:10 says, "Be still, and know that I am God." The Hebrew word for "to be still" is *raphah,* meaning to "cause to fall" or "let go" or "relax."

Psalm 46 describes the time of the end when great earthquakes will shake the earth and the mountains will fall into the sea and the islands will disappear. While this turmoil rages around us, God instructs us to be still, to let go, and relax.

Raphah literally means to open our hand and let something fall. In other words, as we seek the Lord we are simply to let go of our trials, troubles, and problems. We must release our anxieties and our fears.

We also need to seek shelter from the voice of the world. Our society is drugged by noise. Radios blare when no one is listening. Televisions entertain the walls of empty rooms. Teenagers walk around with massive stereo systems propped on one shoulder so they can be surrounded by noise.

People inwardly fear being alone. They don't want to be with themselves. They want their lives filled with activity—with noise. The bedlam they surround themselves with on the outside is indicative of the bedlam on the inside. God wants us to retreat into our prayer closets and leave the noise behind.

Finding a Place of Prayer

Men and women of God in every age have learned to cultivate the discipline of solitude. Moses often climbed into the mountains or entered the tabernacle where he could be alone with the Lord. Daniel secluded himself in his room three times a day to gain strength and wisdom for the demands of being prime minister.

New Testament Christians were no different. The apostle Paul disappeared into Arabia for at least three years, so he could grow in revelation and be taught of the Lord. Peter retreated to the housetop where he could be alone. The apostles said, "Seek out from among you seven men of good reputation, full of the Holy Spirit and wisdom, whom we may appoint over this business; but we will give ourselves continually to prayer and to the ministry of the word" (Acts 6:3,4, NKJV).

You may think you can't carve out any more precious time in your busy schedule to be alone with Jesus. Compare yourself to Susanna Wesley, the mother of John Wesley. She had twenty children living in her small house. You can imagine the bedlam that filled her home.

She knew she needed the Lord's strength, but where could a mother of so many little children find peace and quiet? She worked it out so that when she sat on her chair in the corner and pulled her apron up over her head, all her children were to be quiet. Her communion with Christ helped her to raise a son like John Wesley—the great revivalist.

What does it mean to wait upon the Lord? This portion of Scripture spells it out powerfully:

He gives power to the weak, and to
those who have no might He increases
strength. Even the youths shall faint and
be weary, and the young men shall
utterly fall, but those who wait on the
Lord shall renew their strength; they
shall mount up with wings like eagles,
they shall run and not be weary, they
shall walk and not faint—Isaiah
40:29-31, NKJV.

When you're facing a particularly difficult trial,
God may lead you to spend a lot of extra time in
intercession. Often the best time to pray is in the
middle of the night. Scripture records that *watchings,* or spending time in prayer when a person
would normally be sleeping, was part of Christ's
devotional life. He would go up on a mountain and
pray until early light.

The apostle Paul said he experienced sleepless-
ness many nights. (See 2 Corinthians 11:27.) During watchings you pray effective, fervent prayers
that break through the burdens and yokes that
oppose you.

Our congregation once had a prayer watch for
a woman who was at death's door. Only life-
support equipment was keeping her alive in inten-
sive care, where she lay unconscious. Different
people took turns reading Scripture to her by her

bedside, hoping that her spirit could hear. All night in the waiting room the brethren took turns coming for an hour or two to pray. Back at the church, the elders stayed up all night praying until morning light.

By morning, the woman could sit up, she was conscious, and she began to eat for the first time in about a month. She continued to gain strength until she was back to normal. That was several years ago, and she is still walking mightily in the Lord.

Turning Self Off

As our group of Spirit-filled believers began to seek the Lord during special times of prayer, we recognized the need to engage the enemy in spiritual warfare. It was then that we discovered a new weapon—fasting.

In His Sermon on the Mount, Jesus didn't say, "If you fast . . ." He said, "When you fast . . ." (See Matthew 6:16-18.) God expects His people to fast just as He expects them to give and to pray. He doesn't give us options on any of these disciplines.

Seeing the scriptural mandate for this practice, people in our congregation began to fast. We soon discovered that fasting turned off the strong drives of our soul and body. Normally we take in air to breath, food to eat, and beverages to drink; we have needs for affection, love, and attention; we enjoy the comforts of a house to live in, a bed to sleep in, and nice clothes to wear. Somehow fasting halts at least part of this constant intake.

We found that fasting released our spirit to pray with fervency that resulted in breakthroughs. Fasting wasn't to earn special favor or points with God. Fasting was simply a way of releasing our own spirit to stand before the Spirit of our Father.

As we studied the Scriptures on fasting, we found many types of fasts that were observed for various lengths of time. In a *regular fast,* people gave up eating all foods, but not water. Jesus was on a regular fast when he endured the temptations in the wilderness for forty days.

During an *absolute fast,* people refrained from all food and drink. Before Esther dared to enter the king's presence, she and her maidens took neither food nor drink for three days.

We also discovered the *partial fast,* where only certain foods were off-limits. Daniel participated in a twenty-one day partial fast when he gave up eating meat, drinking alcoholic beverages, and having desserts. He also didn't anoint his face with oil. This was his way of fasting.

What about the motive for fasting? ''Is this not the fast that I have chosen: to loose the bonds of wickedness, to undo the heavy burdens, to let the oppressed go free, and that you break every yoke?'' (Isaiah 58:6, NKJV). We fasted to increase our effectiveness in prayer, or to ''make our voices heard on high.'' (See Isaiah 58:4.)

The Spirit-filled people in the congregation fasted corporately every Tuesday for four and a half years. We believe that their faithfulness and persistence in prayer and fasting are major reasons why we were able to stay close to the Lord and stand in the midst of our trials.

When we relocated to the Christian Outreach Center and started a seminary, new problems awaited us. At the time, the Arch Diocese of St. Louis held the mortgage on the building that housed the Center. Through some unusual circumstances and misunderstandings, we were four payments behind at one point. The Arch Diocese notified us that we had twenty-two days to come up with $28,000 in back payments or the property would revert back to their ownership.

We had no idea where the money would come from. Since the congregation was poor and giving far beyond their means already, we called the church to a twenty-one day Daniel fast. On the nineteenth day of the fast the balance of the money came in, and we were able to pay off what we owed.

Another time we were in terrible financial shape. We trimmed every expense possible and tightened our belts notch by notch. But we still needed a breakthrough from the Lord. Again, we called the congregation to a corporate fast. This time we asked them to fast for a hundred days. Instead of shrinking back and weeping, the people put their heart into it with one accord. On the ninetieth day of our fast, a couple from another part of the country brought a check for $100,000, and the Lord mightily met our needs.

Our church can document many instances when wrestling in the spirit with prayer and fasting affected our corporate life. Tremendous victories have been won.

Do you have a serious problem? Consider fasting as well as praying fervently for the answer. I'm surprised how many people are facing severe marital problems, a runaway teenager, or a debilitating sickness, and they've never considered praying with fasting. When their prayers alone seem to lack fervency and power, I encourage Christians to fast. Fasting does not earn points with God, but it does release your prayer life. I urge you to pour out yourself before God, to be earnest, to be fervent, and to pray *and* fast.

No Ifs, Ands, or Buts

Living in the kingdom of God requires intensity, courage, and daring. The life of faith is not for the faint-hearted or those unwilling to take a risk. Kingdom living can be compared to wrestling, running a race, and fighting a fight. Jesus said, "From the days of John the Baptist until now the kingdom of heaven suffers violence, and the violent take it by force" (Matthew 11:12, NKJV).

Living the kingdom life involves warfare. We discovered that we were not engaged in earthly combat but with war in the heavenlies.

We realized that if our answers didn't come right away we were not to moan, cry, or grow weaker in our requests, but we were to grow stronger and fight harder. We knew we had mighty promises to stand upon and that God's own faithfulness stood behind the promises.

> All things, whatever you ask in prayer, believing, you will receive—Matthew 21:22, NKJV.

> Ask, and it will be given to you; seek, and you will find; knock, and it will be opened to you. For everyone who asks receives, and he who seeks finds, and to him who knocks it will be opened—Luke 11:9,10, NKJV.

There are no ifs, ands, or buts about it. God has made some tremendous promises, and God keeps His word. Christians need to realize that conditions are often connected with the promises of

God, so answered prayer is intertwined with living a life of faith and obedience.

We can't live in sin and expect God to answer us. Scripture teaches, "If I regard iniquity in my heart, the Lord will not hear me" (Psalm 66:18).

As we continued to seek the Lord, He showed us that we had to forgive everybody of everything or the Lord wouldn't hear us. Jesus said in His Sermon on the Mount, "If you do not forgive men their trespasses, neither will your Father forgive your trespasses" (Matthew 6:15, NKJV). If we are cut off from God's forgiveness, we are cut off from everything—including the answers to our prayers.

God taught us much more than forgiveness. We learned to guard our words. When we talked like we weren't going to get answers, we only defeated the purpose of praying. Maintaining a good confession built faith that the answers were on their way.

We also asked God to search our hearts and weed out selfish desires. Most of all, we learned to wrestle with prayer. We had to ask and keep on asking, seek and keep on seeking, knock and keep on knocking.

Holy Intensity

God is an intense God, and He wants His sons and daughters to seek Him intensely. The one who diligently places the kingdom of God above all

other pursuits will find that immeasurable blessings are stored up for him. (See Matthew 6:33.)
God, being a generous Father, wants to bestow
choice blessings upon His children. Do we yearn
to receive as much as He yearns to give? God wants
our heart to become like His heart.

Will we face our problems and difficulties with
the same intensity that God faces them? That holy
intensity does not come from being legalistic or
driving ourselves. As we yield our spirit and our
situation to Him, intensity comes from the drawing and empowering of the Holy Spirit. A holy
intensity is available to any child of God who asks
in faith.

We learned another reason why life in the furnace sometimes can become very intense. Not only
is God intense, but the devil is intensely trying to
stop us.

> Woe to the inhabitants of the earth and
> the sea! For the devil has come down
> to you, having great wrath, because
> he knows that he has a short time—
> Revelation 12:12, NKJV.

Wrath, or *thimon* in the Greek, means to have
swellings of mind or strong passion. *Thimon* does
not necessarily imply being angry but being filled
with a strong passion. Of course, as far as the devil

is concerned, he exercises an angry type of passion toward God's people. He is intently trying to stop and destroy us.

The Lord wants our heart to be fully engaged in the battle. He wants warriors and not weepers. Despite the battles we must not "grow weary while doing good, for in due season we shall reap if we do not lose heart" (Galatians 6:9).

Are you in the furnace? Then don't just have faith. *Fight* the good fight of faith with holy intensity. (See 1 Timothy 6:12; 2 Timothy 4:7.)

CHAPTER FIFTEEN

Rejoicing in the Refiner's Fire

The exodus of the Israelites from Egypt was a monumental miracle. The people had seen all the plagues of God upon Pharaoh and his nation while they themselves were spared. Through the Red Sea they had walked with walls of water standing on either side. Even the sea bottom was dry.

The following day they had seen the bodies of the Egyptian soldiers washed upon the shore. God had destroyed the power of Egypt; they were free at last.

After coming to Mount Sinai, the Israelites received the covenant that Yahweh would be their God and they would be His people. They received His laws and statutes. Then they began their walk to the Promised Land.

Surely the march would not be too difficult, they told themselves. Perhaps it would take several weeks or a month to get there. After all, they did have to travel slowly.

For three days the pillar of fire by night and the cloud by day went before them, leading them straight toward the Promised Land. Then, on the third day, it swerved off to the left. The people wondered but followed. As the days went by they found themselves far away from Canaan.

Days turned into weeks and months. At times the water was scarce, the grass for the cattle was thin, and there seemed to be no food. Stones got in their sandals. The cliffs were hard to climb. The path was more difficult than they had imagined.

Out of the two and a half million or more Jews who left Egypt, only two reached the Land of Promise. What happened? Was it the rigors of the journey? No! The people simply did not rejoice in the furnace. Their murmuring and complaining was the very voice of unbelief—and God slew them. God wanted them to walk through the wilderness rejoicing. Amazingly, rejoicing in the midst of trials is the key for coming through them.

Moses told the people again and again to rejoice. David quoted Moses when he said,

> Let the righteous be glad; let them rejoice before God: yea, let them exceedingly rejoice. Sing unto God, sing praises to his name: extol him that rideth upon the heavens by his name JAH, and rejoice before him—Psalm 68:3,4.

This was the way they were to march across the stones and sand, through the dry desert. They were to face the scarcity of food and water with rejoicing. This was how they were to deal with every problem along the way. But instead of rejoicing, they murmured.

If we do not walk through our wilderness rejoicing, we will not enter into the promised land of strength and rest. Murmuring is the expression of doubting while rejoicing is the expression of faith. In fact, rejoicing creates the very atmosphere for faith to grow.

Robbed of Joy

The prophet Joel foretold how the blessings of God upon His people would be completely eaten up through the centuries. The prophet said that all the blessings were eaten up "because *joy* is withered away from the sons of men" (Joel 1:12, italics added). Sounds backward, doesn't it? The people didn't lose their joy because the blessings were taken away, but the blessings eluded them when they lost their joy.

Like Israel in the wilderness, our fathers in the early church lost their blessings when they lost their joy. During the Dark Ages the church almost died in the wilderness. Even today the philosophy of churches often robs people of joy. Being "reverent" often means not smiling too much in church. People will think you're frivolous or not paying attention.

I remember a story about a family that was driving to church one bright Sunday morning. They were laughing and having a good time in the car, talking about the picnic lunch they had planned that afternoon. When they got out of the car, they were happy and bubbling. But as they approached the church, their faces changed, and a quiet, somber look came over their countenances. One of the children was still acting joyful and happy. The mother turned and scolded, "Shh! We're going into church now; be quiet."

Throughout the service this family sat quietly and piously, thinking that their attitude pleased God. They sang beautiful hymns and recited lovely phrases. With cordial smiles on their faces they shook hands with the pastor at the door. Then they walked out, climbed in the car, and after a minute or so, they began to relax. Breathing a sigh of relief, they began to smile and be joyful again.

This type of depressing scene happens countless times every Sunday. What happens in our churches? What kind of teaching, philosophy, and traditions have robbed our churches of joy?

Many people express joy only at football games or parties. If we are cheerful or lighthearted as we attend to the regular activities of everyday life, we're considered abnormal. But being cheerful is what God wants. Life should be a time of rejoicing, no matter what the wilderness or the struggle, because we live our lives in Christ.

Most people are not usually grumbling or murmuring in their walk, but they're not rejoicing either. They're just taking their lumps, gritting their teeth, and steeling themselves to endure. They may not be giving up, but they feel far from God and have no real sense of spiritual victory.

A Rejoicing Heart

In studying the Psalms you'll find that rejoicing is the highest form of praise. Praise is the highest form of worship, which is one of the highest acts for a child of God. The best way to praise God continually is simply to rejoice in your walk wherever you are.

A rejoicing heart says, "God, You've made everything all right. No matter what my trials are, I think You and what You're doing are tremendous. You really make me happy." That is high praise.

That's why the apostle Paul told the early Christians to "Rejoice in the Lord always. Again I will say, rejoice" (Philippians 4:4, NKJV). Paul did this even in the face of death.

Peter said to "rejoice to the extent that you partake of Christ's sufferings" (1 Peter 4:12,13, NKJV).

Jesus said, "Blessed are you when they revile and persecute you . . . Rejoice and be exceedingly glad" (Matthew 5:11,12, NKJV).

By rejoicing in the midst of the furnace, we voice our trust in God to see us through. Our hearts well up to meet His.

The world warns us of emotionalism, and there *is* reason to be cautious. We should not let our emotions rule us. We want Christ, working through our will, to rule us. We do not want to lose control in an emotional state just for the kick it gives us. That is rejoicing in the flesh.

On the other hand, we shouldn't keep our joy hidden behind a solemn face and say, "I have my joy deep down inside." The Scriptures clearly state that joy must be expressed. And when joy is expressed, it will show on your face.

In Psalms 68:3, David said, "Let the righteous be *glad*." The Hebrew word for glad is *sameach,* which means "to make merry" or "to express joy"! We are to work at it. We are to show it on our faces and in our actions.

In Psalms 40:16, David said, "Let all those that seek thee *rejoice* and be glad in thee." Here the word for rejoice is *sus* or *sis,* which means "to make mirth" or literally "to go from one degree of joy to another," "to go higher and higher in joy." This means that you pump it up in a sense or allow it to spring forth.

This does not mean to work yourself into an emotional lather. But, if you come home after having had a rough day and you're not feeling very joyful, you can begin to think about why you should be joyful. Begin to talk joyously of the Lord. Gradually your heart will be released, and soon you will be honestly rejoicing before God. This is not being hypocritical. Rejoicing allows your will to make a decision to be happy until your feelings can catch up.

Jumping for Joy

Are you open about expressing your joy in a scriptural manner? David also said, "Let them *rejoice* before God" (Psalm 68:3, italics added). An entirely different Hebrew word is used in this verse. *Alats* means "to dance" or "jump for joy." We are to jump and leap before the Lord, even as David leaped before the ark of the covenant as it was carried into Jerusalem.

David's wife Michal thought her husband's behavior was undignified, but it was *her* attitude that was not pleasing to God. The focal point of God's presence—the ark of the covenant—was coming to live next door to David's palace. What a blessing. What a high honor. But Michal couldn't see it. She wasn't spiritually fit to rule with David, and he had her sent away.

But where is the ark of the covenant now? God's presence still dwells in His temple. Aren't you now the temple of God? The focal point of God's presence is even closer than being next door. If David had something to leap and dance about then, you and I really have something to rejoice in today. Real "reverence" is doing it God's way. Revering Him includes obeying Him.

Rejoicing in God includes other facets, too. Psalms 81:1 says we are to make a *joyful noise* unto the Lord. The Hebrew word is *rua,* which means "to shout loudly for joy." To some this may not seem very dignified, but it is God's way.

Lest anyone be led away in the flesh to sinful emotionalism, let me give a simple spiritual guideline about what the limits are. Do not let the physical activity (clapping, shouting, dancing, etc.) distract or drown out the spiritual activity. The words of worship and praise must be enhanced by the physical acts, not over-ridden. Rejoicing can be extremely physical and still be a true expression of our human spirit's praise to God.

For instance, Psalms 149:2 says that the children of Zion are to be *joyful* in their King. Here the word is *gil* or *gul* in the Hebrew, meaning "to pirouette, to spin around." That certainly does not sound like the kind of worship services to which we are accustomed. Most churches don't come within a country mile of such worship. They say it isn't dignified. But who is the author of dignity? Isn't it the Lord?

But wasn't that in the Old Testament? Weren't they a little fanatical in those days? Well, let's look in the New Testament at Jesus Himself.

After the seventy came back and reported to Jesus about their preaching trips, "In that hour Jesus *rejoiced* in spirit" (Luke 10:21, italics added). Here the Greek word for rejoicing is *agalliao,* which means literally "to leap much for joy."

When they came back and reported all the wonderful things that had happened, Jesus, the perfect Son of God, our dignified Leader, began to leap much for joy. What a sight! How it must have pleased the Father. But would we let Him in our churches? Can you see what we've lost through the traditions of men?

It Pays to Rejoice

Richard Wurmbrand, the pastor who was tortured for fourteen years in communist prisons, told a story about spending time in solitary confinement. After having been there for three months, he was very weak. His captors provided him with only a loaf of bread for his weekly ration of food. As he laid there on his cot, he was trying to remember the sermon of Jesus in Luke 6.

Wurmbrand could remember that in times of persecution Jesus had said, "Blessed are ye, when men shall hate you, and when they shall separate you from their company, and shall reproach you, and shall cast out your name as evil, for the Son of man's sake" (Luke 6:22). What a furnace!

He had done that, but was there not something else Jesus said to do? For a while his mind struggled to remember, and then it came. Jesus had also said, "Rejoice in that day and leap for joy" (Luke 6:22, NKJV).

I have rejoiced, but I have not leaped for joy, he thought. So with what strength he could muster, he got slowly up from his cot and began to do little leaps and weak shouts for joy before God there in his cell. As he continued, his praise grew stronger. As the guard outside looked through the little peep hole, he thought Wurmbrand was going crazy.

The communists did not want any adverse publicity about this famous prisoner, so the guard came in and tried to calm him down. But Pastor Wurmbrand was so happy in the Lord that he could not stop. At that point the guard rushed out again. In about fifteen minutes he came back with a tray loaded with cheeses, meats, breads, and fruit for him to eat. Wurmbrand learned one of God's lessons: "It pays to rejoice the way God told you to rejoice," he said.

In the midst of the fiery furnace we are to leap and dance around as Shadrach, Meshach, and

Abednego must have done. If we do this, something wonderful will begin to happen in our lives. We will be set free and not even the smell of the smoke will be on us. The only things that will burn away are the bonds that bind us.

The Blessings of Rejoicing

In rejoicing you will find endurance in the midst of the furnace. For the joy that was set before Him, Jesus endured the cross—that horrible torture where the wrath of God and the wrath of man met in Jesus Christ. He endured both, paying that awful price for our sins. What held Him up? He endured ''for the joy that was set before Him'' (Hebrews 12:2). You, too, will be able to endure your crosses with joy.

The blessings do not stop here. Soon other wonderful blessings will be worked in you. You will develop patience.

> My brethren, count it all joy when you fall into various trials, knowing that the testing of your faith produces patience. But let patience have its perfect work, that you may be perfect and complete, lacking nothing—James 1:2,3, NKJV.

After patience has done her work, three great things will have been developed in you.

You will be "perfect." Oh, how we yearn to be perfect!

You will be "complete." You will be a whole person; you won't have any big empty gaps in your personality or makeup.

Finally, *you will "lack nothing."* All things will be in place. Everything you need and want will be there when you have come through the furnace with joy.

Rejoicing is the key to many victories. Those demonic attacks that may grip your life need not be there. The way to fight demons is not to go around rebuking them all the time, although there is a time for that. The way to fight them is to go around rejoicing all the time. Psalm 81 describes a rejoicing man of God; and verse 9 says, "there shall no strange god be in thee." Both Moses and the apostle Paul point out that these strange gods were actually demons. (See Deuteronomy 32:17; 1 Corinthians 10:20.)

Giving God Joy

In our local charismatic group, every day someone reported another setback. Sometimes so many reports would come in over a period of a week that if we were not careful we would get discouraged and downcast. Then someone would say, "Let us rejoice," and we knew what they meant.

We began to sing and clap our hands. Soon we might even be dancing before the Lord. Looking back, we can see the problems were all taken care of, and we became much stronger because of the adversities we faced. Those burdens that tried to break us were always broken instead.

Despite praying for the people and trying to be in tune with the Lord, I sometimes felt spiritually dry before I was to minister publicly. I used to worry and even panic about whether or not the message I was preaching was going to come out all right. I wondered if the people would be blessed. Then I learned that the joy of the Lord was my strength. (See Nehemiah 8:10.)

Now before I speak before any group or at a conference, I get alone with the Lord in the quiet of my room. I may turn on a tape of Christian music, or I may rejoice without it. I begin to sing and clap my hands to the Lord. Finally, I might even find myself dancing all around the room having a tremendous time with Jesus. My spirit opens up, and the blessings and anointing of God flow in. By the time I get to the meeting, I find myself ready to go, and the power of God moves mightily in the service.

While rejoicing in the Lord brings us many blessings, you may be surprised to learn that *God* rejoices, too! This amazing passage has been a real delight to me.

> The Lord thy God in the midst of thee
> is mighty; he will save, he will rejoice
> over thee with joy; he will rest in his
> love, he will joy over thee with
> singing—Zephaniah 3:17.

The God of all the universe is joyous over *us!* His love is so satisfied because it has found a resting place in us. The Lord literally goes "from one degree of joy over us to another" (sus) with a "mirthful gladness" (sameach), and He "leaps" and "spins around" (gul) over us with singing.

What a thrill to be loved like that! I never could have imagined that God felt that way about me. Now I rejoice in Him.

How Hot and How Long?

A joyful spirit brings even more joy. Rejoicing breeds rejoicing in an upward spiral. What an easy way to be an overcomer. Praise the Lord for the furnace that produces pure gold in our lives.

The Master Refiner uses a variety of tests, trials, and temptations to accomplish His work in our lives. He knows exactly how hot to fire the furnace. How long does He keep us there? That depends on our response to the flames.

Rejoicing in the midst of the Refiner's fire demonstrates trust and faith in His plan for our lives. Why does He allow these trials?

> That the genuineness of your faith,
> being much more precious than gold
> that perishes, though it is tested by fire,
> may be found to praise, honor, and glory
> at the revelation of Jesus Christ—1 Peter
> 1:7, NKJV.

Remember that the work God accomplishes in our lives will last for eternity. No wonder He lingers so long over us. Every shred of selfishness, every haughty attitude, every scrap of jealousy—all will be consumed in the Refiner's fire. When He finally gazes into the golden, molten liquid of our lives, He will see only a reflection of Himself.

And we will know—without a doubt—that "our light affliction, which is but for a moment, is working for us a far more exceeding and eternal weight of glory" (2 Corinthians 4:17, NKJV). Every battle, every test, every tribulation will be worth the end result when we stand in His glorious presence on that final day.

About The Author

After completing his tour in the Army, Bob Heil received a degree in Geological Engineering from the University of Kansas and Bachelor and Master of Divinity degrees from Concordia Seminary, Springfield, Illinois. He since has received his Doctor of Theology degree from the International Bible College and Theological Seminary.

For ten years Dr. Bob Heil was a Lutheran pastor to several congregations in Missouri. When he left the parish ministry, Bob began a walk of faith as a full-time teacher in the Body of Christ at large. He has spoken at seminars, clinics, conventions, and congregations across the nation and around the world.

Dr. Heil is founder of the Christian Outreach School of Ministries where he was president and teacher for several years. In addition he was director of the Christian Outreach Center in Hillsboro, Missouri, which serves as a church, a family Bible camp, and a center for additional training of Spirit-filled pastors. The Center is also a focal point for the worldwide work of the Bible and Literacy League with over 300 missionaries and other workers. Dr. Heil is also an International Advisor at large for Women's Aglow Fellowship. Bob is married and has four children.

Through the ministry of Praise The Lord Fellowship, Dr. Heil directs the International Leadership Training Institute. Their three year curriculum is designed so that indigenous leaders in the communist and Third World countries can receive full seminary level training without leaving their fields or factories. Those successfully completing the program receive degrees from the Christian Outreach School of Ministries and Christ The King University. The program will also be offered in the West.

If you would like more information on this program or a listing of Bob Heil's teaching tapes, you may contact him at:

Praise The Lord Fellowship
2086 Teakwood Drive
Columbus, OH 43229